Then Sings My Soul

Then Sings My Soul

Studies in the Psalms

Vol. 1, First Collection

M. Dean Koontz

iUniverse, Inc.

New York Lincoln Shanghai

Then Sings My Soul
Studies in the Psalms

iUniverse books may be ordered through booksellers or by contacting:

iUniverse
2021 Pine Lake Road, Suite 100
Lincoln, NE 68512
www.iuniverse.com
1-800-Authors (1-800-288-4677)

Because of the dynamic nature of the Internet, any Web addresses or links contained in this book may have changed since publication and may no longer be valid.

The views expressed in this work are solely those of the author and do not necessarily reflect the views of the publisher, and the publisher hereby disclaims any responsibility for them.

ISBN: 978-0-595-47171-3 (pbk)
ISBN: 978-0-595-91451-7 (ebk)

Printed in the United States of America

"Then sings my soul,

My Savior God, to Thee;

How great Thou art,

How great Thou art!"

Stuart K. Hine

Contents

Preface

For many years, I have followed a pattern of reading through the Psalms every month at a pace of 5 chapters per day. This means, of course, that the Psalms can be read 12 times in a year. As a pastor for almost 50 years, I have outlined and preached through many of the psalms, first finding a rich storehouse of treasure for my own heart, and then sharing it with my people, who, I pray, have had a little rub off from me to enrich and bless their heart as well.

A few years ago, I picked up a paper in the Denver Seminary Study Series by Robert Alden, Professor of Old Testament. Dr. Alden is an acquaintance that I greatly admire for his scholarship and Christian commitment. Being an early graduate of the Seminary, I did not have the opportunity to sit under his instruction, since he came to the faculty after my time there. I served on the Board of Directors for 10 years, and got to know him casually during my visits to the campus. I mention this because he has contributed, in some measure, to my putting this collection of psalm studies together in book form.

The purpose of his study was to show how to find themes and outlines within the psalms, themes and outlines that are integral with the psalms rather than imposed on them. And he spoke of a number of abuses to which the Bible is put in sermon making.

"There is the sermon that starts with a verse or passage and never returns to it; the scripture portion becomes the opening illustration rather than the basis of the message. A second variety is like the first; the scripture is used to illustrate the message other than at the beginning. The Bible and in particular the narrative portions of the Old Testament become a source book for anecdotes and pictures of speech. A third type is the proof-texting type of sermon. In it the sin of quoting out of context is committed most frequently. Contexts are ignored and the purpose of the biblical author is often severely contorted. A fourth abuse is to assume there is no doctrine or gospel in the psalms and simply ignore them. This is the most unpardonable of abuses. Another view assumes there is no application of certain psalms or portions of them to the modern believer and therefore they are unpreachable." (Seminary Study Series, "Making Sermons From The Psalms, by Robert L. Alden, Denver Seminary (1979), page 1)

Following retirement a few years ago, one of my goals was to gather together my various study projects in the hope that eventually I could put them in a form that would be beneficial to a wider audience, possibly through publication. In my years of pastoral ministry, I had preached on the psalms many times, seeking to outline them first, and then to build a study or a message on the outline. Dr. Alden, in his paper, gave me the idea of pulling together these many years of personal meditation in the psalm in some systematic form. Many, of course, have written meditations on the psalms that have been published. Some of the more recent books on the psalms pick out certain psalms for study, while omitting others. I wanted to go through the psalms in a systematic way, without omissions. My plan, which, I confess, is a somewhat monumental undertaking, is to put together 5 collections of 30 psalms each. What follows is the first collection, Psalms 1-30. I include for each of the psalms, first the full text, then an outline, and finally, an exposition.

I have been blessed by reading the insights of others, but putting something together that I can call my own, for reasons I shall not go into here, satisfies a deep need within me. It also fosters in me a desire to share my discoveries with other treasure seekers. I hope I can join the many who have raised precious nuggets of truth to the surface, so that they lie there for all seekers after truth to gather and store away in the chambers of the heart for personal enrichment and blessing.

Dean Koontz

Psalm 1

"The Truly Happy Man"

Psalm 1

1 Blessed is the man who does not
      walk in the counsel of the wicked
      or stand in the way of sinners
      or sit in the seat of mockers.

2 But his delight is in the law of the Lord,
      and on his law he meditates day and night.

3 He is like a tree planted by streams of water,
      which yields its fruit in season and
      whose leaf does not wither.
      Whatever he does prospers.

4 Not so the wicked!
      They are like chaff
      that the wind blows away.

5 Therefore the wicked will not stand in the judgment
      nor sinners in the assembly of the righteous.

6 For the Lord watches over the way of the righteous,
      but the way of the wicked will perish.

(NIV)

Psalm 1

The Truly Happy Man

True happiness is never an end in itself, but comes as a by-product to the one who submits to the will of God and is obedient to the Word of God.

I. The Righteous Man—He Trusts In The Lord. *"Blessed is the man who trusts in the Lord" (Jeremiah 17:7).*

A. Not conformed to this world.

1. Accepting its advice—*"does not **walk** in the counsel of the wicked"*
2. Approving its actions—*"does not **stand** in the way of sinners"*
3. Adopting its attitudes—*"does not **sit** in the seat of mockers (scoffers) (v 1)*

B. But transformed by the Word. Whatever shapes a man's thinking shapes his life.

1. Delighting in the law of the Lord regularly *"His delight is in the law of the Lord ..."*
2. Meditating on the law of the Lord continually *"day and night" (v 2)*

C. And formed to do His will. *"He is like a tree ..."*

1. Vitality—*" planted by streams of water"*
2. Productivity—*"which yields its fruit in season"*
3. Longevity—*"whose leaf does not wither"*
4. Prosperity—*"whatever he does prospers (v 6)*

II. The Wicked Man—He Trusts In Man. *"Cursed is the man who trusts in mankind and makes flesh his strength, and whose heart turns away from the Lord" (Jeremiah 17:5).*

    A. Cursed. *"They are like chaff that the wind blows away" (v 4)*

        1. Rootless
        2. Weightless
        3. Useless

    B. Condemned. *"They will not stand in the judgment, ("not a leg to stand on")*
    C. Alienated. *"nor sinners in the assembly of the righteous"*

III. The Two Way—Summarized.

    A. The way of the righteous. *"The Lord watches over (knows) the way of the righteous"*
    B. The way of the wicked. *"the way of the wicked will perish" (v 6)*

Psalm 1

The Truly Happy Man

The happiness that we all seek, in one way or another, does not come because we have been seeking happiness for happiness sake, but in seeking God, our unshakeable happy God, who because He is sovereign is never frustrated by any lack. In knowing Him, and loving Him, and obeying Him, we find our greatest joy and pleasure. John Piper in his insightful book *Desiring God* reminds us that

> "The happiness of God in God is the foundation of our happiness in God. If God did not joyfully uphold and display his glory, the ground of our joy would be gone. God's pursuit of praise from us and our pursuit of pleasure in him are in perfect harmony. For God is most glorified in us when we are most satisfied in him." (Desiring God by John Piper, page 50)

So happiness isn't something we actively seek, but is a by-product of delighting in God.

Here in this introductory psalm, David is telling us the same thing—that happiness comes from the decision to submit our will to the will of God and to be obedient to the word of God. He defines for us what Jesus meant by the man who takes the narrow way as opposed to the man who follows the broad way. A person's decision to follow God, Jesus says, defines the direction his life will take, and determines the destiny at which he will ultimately arrive.

Jeremiah, in a parallel passage to Psalm 1, says that the righteous man is happy or blessed because he *"trusts in the Lord" (Jeremiah 17:7)*, while the wicked man is cursed, because he *"trusts in mankind and makes flesh his strength, and whose heart turns away from the Lord" (Jeremiah 17:5)*.

Let's examine more closely Psalm 1 and seek to discover anew what David considers to be the secret of true happiness.

The Happy Man is the Righteous Man

A righteous man is one who desires to live life as God meant it to be lived when He created us in His own image and likeness. Life lived rightly in accordance with His word and will is, first of all....

A Life Not Conformed To This World

First, it is a life that is not conformed to this world's standards. The psalmist says the righteous man doesn't accept the world's *advice.* He *"does not walk in the counsel of the wicked."* Oh, there are plenty of worldly advisors out there telling us what constitutes worldly happiness, the amount of *power* that you wield, the number of *possessions* you have accumulated, and the variety of *pleasures* you have experienced. The psalmist warns us not to be drawn into the wrong kind of worldly input of wicked advisors. With the number of clamant cries from every side, this is not as easy as it might seem. Our peril, as believers, is that we get infected by "the world's slow stain" before we know what is happening, so that what we would have deplored a few years before, we now accept. It is the old frog-in-the-frying-pan syndrome. The frog just sits there and eventually boils, because the heat is turned up slowly and imperceptibly.

Then, too, we are not to approve of worldly *actions* or life-styles. The righteous man *"does not stand in the way of sinners."* We are told not "to stand in" but to "stand against" the way of the world. To be sure we have to live *in* the world, but we do not have to be *of* the world. We can be loving and tolerant of a worldly person, for instance, without being tolerant of that worldly person's behavior. This subtle distinction is often unrecognized by the worldly man, and the Christian is often accused of intolerance when he refuses to accept what a person does, although he may accept what that person is, one who is loved by God and made in His image.

And again, the righteous man, one who trusts in the Lord, doesn't adopt the world's *attitudes.* He *"does not sit in the seat of mockers or scoffers."* A careful reading of the psalm reveals that there is a progression intended here. First "walk" then "stand" and finally "sit." A choice to sin, may proceed, if unchecked, to becoming a habit, we *stand* in sin; and finally that habit can develop into a settled way of life, we *sit* continuously bound by and helpless in that sinful pattern. The same progression is seen in the nouns 'wicked', 'sinner', and 'scoffer'. If one flirts with sin, there is a chance that he may become enslaved by sin! How does the old adage go?

> Sow a thought,
> reap an act;
> Sow an act,
> reap a habit;
> Sow a habit,
> reap a character;
> Sow a character,
> Reap a destiny.

"God cannot be mocked." We reap what we sow.

A Life Transformed By The Word

The psalmist moves to the positive, and tells us what the righteous man does do to ensure a happy consequence to his choices. He isn't conformed to the world, but the Word transforms him. Whatever shapes a man's thinking shapes his life. The proverb reminds us that we are becoming what we think. *"Delighting in the law of the Lord,"* reflects an expectant *attitude* of heart, while *"meditating on the law day and night"* reveals a consistent *action* on our part. If we do not love his Word, we will not read it; if we do not delight in it, we will not want to do what it says. The proper attitudes and actions that should characterize our thought of God's Word are repeatedly described for us in the longest psalm, Psalm 119. When the Word of God becomes the *"joy and rejoicing of our hearts,"* then it transforms us. That must be what Paul is referring to when he says in Romans 12 verse 2, *"Do not conform any longer to the pattern of this world, but be transformed by the renewing of your mind."* Mind renewal is accomplished through meditating on the Word of God.

A Life Formed To Do God's Will

The psalmist goes on to tell us what the expected result will be of the choice to seek God's Word and to submit to His will. Spiritual formation takes place. This man will be *"like a tree …"*

Such a life has *stability*. It is *"planted by streams of water …"* The roots go deep. It is nourished by hidden springs. We need that something underground, not visible to the eye, the roots. What roots are to the tree, what rest is to the body, what peace is to the home, what depth is to an ocean, nothing in heaven above or earth beneath can compare with it. Only a stable life can be a productive life. Jesus talks about building life on a strong foundation, so that when the storms of life sweep in, we will still stand strong before wind and wave.

And it is characterized by *productivity*. It *"yields its fruit in season."* Every strong life is characterized by rootage and fruitage, receptivity and activity. Many of us need that double emphasis.

Such a life also has *longevity*. *"Whose leaf does not wither."* I suspect that is what the psalmist means in Psalm 92 verses 14 and 15: *"The righteous ... will flourish ... and grow ... they will still bear fruit in old age, they will stay fresh and green, proclaiming, 'The Lord is upright; He is my Rock, and there is no wickedness in Him.'"* Jeremiah's comment is *"... he never fails to bear fruit"* (17:8). That is certainly something to which we ought to aspire!

Finally, it is a life characterized by *prosperity*. *"Whatever he does prospers."* I doubt seriously whether this is material prosperity that is in view (although such a life tends even to a better outlook economically). It certainly means spiritually. Spiritual prosperity means being rich toward God, finding our Source of supply in Him.

Now let's review briefly what is said of the wicked man.

The Unhappy Man is the Wicked Man

Many psalms say that the wicked man may do well in this life according to the world's standard of success. Sometimes it seems that he has everything going for him, and no calamity seems to befall him. At times this is a real problem for the psalmist, and he isn't shy about saying so. But God doesn't pay all of His accounts in this life. Those who trust in man, make flesh their strength, and turn away from the Lord, are cursed by God (Jeremiah 17:5). They will be like *"chaff that the wind blows away"* (v 4). Jeremiah's description is very graphic, *"He will be like a bush in the desert and will not see when prosperity comes, but will live in stony wastes in the wilderness, a land of salt without inhabitant"* (17:6). All of us who have traveled in the Southwest have seen the tumbleweed blowing across the highway sometimes creating a real traffic hazard. The tumbleweed is rootless, almost weightless and useless. That's a description of the man who leaves God out of his life.

"They will not stand in the judgment." In other words, they will not have "a leg to stand on" when they stand **condemned** before God.

And they will not take their place in the assembly of the righteous. They are **alienated** from the presence of God forever. What an awful thing to contemplate!

The Two Ways Summarized

The psalmist summarizes these two ways in the closing verse, *"The Lord watches over (knows) the way of the righteous, but the way of the wicked will perish."* Proverbs 10:25 is also an apt summary, *"When the storm has swept by, the wicked are gone, but the righteous stand firm forever."*

The criteria for determining a happy life and a happy ending to life is going God's way, doing God's will, and trusting God's word. Any other course is doomed to frustration and failure.

> *"Lord, I want to live my life righteously, that is, live it in the way that you planned for me to live it—doing the right thing, going the right way. Your Word instructs me in that way. Help me to delight in it and meditate on it continuously. Let me find the refreshing wellspring of life therein so that my life, like a well watered tree, will produce the fruit of righteousness daily."*

Something to Ponder

1. There are two kinds of people in the world, the righteous and the wicked. All lives are like trees, for good or ill. There are good trees that produce good fruit and bad trees that produce bad fruit. Jesus said, a person is known by the fruit he bears. And a tree that produces no fruit has somehow lost the reason for its existence.

2. The Proverbs tell us that it is possible for our lives to be "trees of life" to the world. A person of wisdom is a "tree of life" embraced by many and a blessing to all who partake (Proverbs 3:18). The fruit of righteousness is a "tree of life" (Proverbs 11:30) Here the fruit is souls won for Christ, those pointed to their true Source of Life. When our longing heart finds fulfillment, we become a "tree of life" to other longing hearts (Proverbs 13:12).

Psalm 2

"Kings and Things"

Psalm 2

1 Why do the nations conspire
    and the peoples plot in vain?

2 The kings of the earth take their stand
    and the rulers gather together against the LORD
    and against his Anointed One.

3 "Let us break their chains," they say,"
    and throw off their fetters."

4 The One enthroned in heaven laughs;
    the Lord scoffs at them.

5 Then he rebukes them in his anger
    and terrifies them in his wrath, saying,

6 "I have installed my King on Zion, my holy hill."

7 I will proclaim the decree of the LORD: He said to me,
    "You are my Son; today I have become your Father.

8. Ask of me, and I will make the nations your inheritance,
    the ends of the earth your possession.

9 You will rule them with an iron scepter;
    you will dash them to pieces like pottery."

10 Therefore, you kings, be wise;
    be warned, you rulers of the earth.

11 Serve the LORD with fear and rejoice with trembling.

12 Kiss the Son, lest he be angry and you be destroyed in your way,
    for his wrath can flare up in a moment.

Blessed are all who take refuge in him.

NIV

Psalm 2

Kings and Things

I. The Kings of the Earth. *"The kings of the earth take their stand, and the rulers gather together against the Lord and against his Anointed One" (v 2).*

> **A. The nations are angry.** *"Why do the nations conspire (in an uproar) and the peoples plot in vain?" (v 1).*
> **B. Their anger is directed against the Lord.** It is ... *"Against the Lord and against His Anointed One (Messiah)" (v .2).*
> **C. They refuse to submit; they want to be free.** *"Let us break their chains,"* they say, *"and throw off their fetters" (v 3).*

II. The King of The Universe. *"The One enthroned in heaven laughs"*

> **A. He scoffs at them.** *"The Lord scoffs at them" (v 4).*
> **B. He is angry with them.** *"Then he rebukes them in his anger and terrifies them in his wrath ..." (v 5)*
> **C He speaks to them.** *"But as for Me, I have installed My King on Zion, My holy hill" (v 6).*

III. The King of Kings. *"You will rule them with an iron scepter; you will dash them to pieces like pottery" (v 9).*

> **A. The Son Speaks.** *"I will proclaim the decree of the Lord: He said to me, "You are my Son; today I have become your Father." (v 7).*
> **B. The Father Speaks.** *"Ask of me, and I will make the nations your inheritance, the ends of the earth your possession" (v 8).*
> **C. Warning to the kings.** *"Therefore, you kings, be wise; be warned, you rulers of the earth. Serve the Lord with fear and rejoice with trembling. Kiss the Son, lest he be angry and you be destroyed in your way, for his wrath can flare up in a moment" (v 10-12).*

1. Serve the Lord
   2. Kiss the Son
      3. Take refuge in Him

"Blessed are all who take refuge in him" (v 12)

Psalm 2

Kings and Things

Psalm 2 opens with a great conspiracy. Nations, peoples, kings and rulers plot together to throw off the rule of God, and establish their own independence from His sovereign control. This is certainly nothing new? It has been going on since the beginning of time.

The older interpreters referred this Psalm to David, and although he was probably referring to some local and temporal event unknown to us, these are swallowed up in the universal and the eternal. The psalm is unquestionably Messianic. Down through the ages there has been a "jihad" against God and His people by the kings of the nations, and behind them has lurked the fallen archangel, Lucifer, seeking to overthrow the sovereign rule of God and direct allegiance to himself. And this will reach its climax at the end of the age when, *"the kings of the earth will gather together to make war against the King of kings and Lord of lords" and He will strike them with the sharp sword out of His mouth, and "rule them with an iron scepter" (Revelation 19:15-19).*

Consider first,

The Kings of the Earth

"The kings of the earth take their stand and the rulers gather together against the Lord and against his Anointed One" (vs. 2).

Notice the extent of their rebellion-"nations", "peoples", "kings", and "rulers". The Old Testament is a commentary on those nations that have aligned themselves against God and Israel, the nation He chose to be a repository of His truth and a channel for the Messiah. Egypt, Assyria, Babylon, Medo-Persia, Greece, and Rome tried unsuccessfully to destroy the people of God. Today, some of those ancient empires are replicated in Egypt, Syria, Iraq and Iran, who are avowed enemies of the Jewish state. The Apocalypse speaks of a Ten Nation confederacy corresponding to the ten toes of Daniel's end-time vision, headed by a sinister Beast out of the Abyss, the Antichrist figure, demonized and energized by The Dragon, Satan, and assisted by the False Prophet, who will persecute God's people and lead the armies of the world against the Anointed One of God-the Christ. That is when this Psalm finds its ultimate fulfillment.

Their determination is obvious. It is *deliberate*. *"They take counsel (conspire) …"* They devise strategies and schemes to overthrow the rule of God. It is *united*. *"They take counsel together … gather together …"* It is *determined*. *"They set themselves (take their stand) …"* like Goliath took his stand (same word) to defy the host of Israel. It has ever been the cry of the nations, *"We will not have this man to reign over us" (Luke 19:14)*.

And what is their reason for revolt? They want to be totally free from God's so-called "chains" and "fetters." The yoke that to the true believer is "easy" and "light" is to the blind and self-willed as "bands" and "cords" which they are eager to cast off. They perpetuate the sin of our first parents, desiring to do as they please rather than what pleases God.

The psalm begins with the question, "Why?" *"Why do the nations conspire etc."* No satisfactory answer is forthcoming. Why does the human heart reject the God who made him in His image and likeness and loves with an everlasting love? It is totally unreasonable. Christ, God's Anointed, is the Righteous King, the Desire of the nations. Where He rules, righteousness flows down, blessings abound. It is useless. It is "vain." By virtue of His atoning work and resurrection, Christ has become King of kings, and He shall reign forever and ever. The Church may be oppressed but never suppressed. And God shall at length cover all Christ's enemies with confusion and ruin.

The King of the Universe

He Scoffs At Them

"The One enthroned in heaven laughs; the Lord scoffs at them" (vs. 4). God laughs while kings rage! He has the last laugh, as it were. It is God that sets the bounds of nations, and grants kings the authority to rule. They are dependent on His authority, and are ordained *"to punish those who do wrong and to praise those who do right" (I Peter 2:14)*. So the nations are limited in their power and authority, but it is this very limitation that is galling to them. Since governments exercise power, they get the idea that they can make their own laws and pursue their own policies that please them rather than God. It is their desire to be totalitarian in their exercise of authority. But since God grants the charter for their existence, governments can never wrest the control away from a sovereign God. God is not fazed by their conspiracy. He is unthreatened. He is

secure in His throne rights as Universal Sovereign. He laughs at their puny efforts, seeing them as "a drop in the bucket."

He Is Angry With Them

"Then he rebukes them in his anger and terrifies them in his wrath …" (v 5). History should teach a valuable lesson to kings and nations. God has raised them up, and overthrown them. Certainly God taught Nebuchadnezzar of Babylon that lesson when he caused him to go temporarily insane and made him like a beast of the field until he realized his proper place in the scheme of things and his relationship to the Sovereign God of the universe.

He Speaks To Them

And to demonstrate His right, He chooses to enthrone His own ruler, His Son: *"You are my Son, today I have begotten you" (v. 7).* This Anointed One would rule in a special way for God, committed to serving Him and carrying out His will.

All the kings of Israel and Judah were supposed to carry out that mandate, but they did not. A few select kings of Judah like David, Solomon, Asa, Jehoshaphat, Hezekiah, and Josiah sought to obey God, but none of them did so completely. But God has His True King whose kingdom will have no end, whose rule will be righteous. The time is coming when *"the kingdom of the world has become the kingdom of our Lord and of His Christ, and He shall reign for ever and ever" (Revelation 11:15).*

"I have installed my King on Zion, my holy hill" (v. 6).

The King of All Kings

The Son Speaks

Here the voice changes, and the Son speaks. *"He said to me, 'You are my Son; today I have become your Father'" (v. 7).* God said this concerning Solomon, *"I will establish his kingdom forever. I will be his father, and he will be my son" (2 Samuel 7:14).* And the promise included the normal interaction of father with son, correction and affirmation. Psalm 110 emphasizes that this took place when *"The Lord says to my Lord: 'Sit at my right hand until I make your enemies a footstool for your feet'" (v 1).* Jesus is Everlasting King, Everlasting Priest, and everlasting Prophet, our ruler, redeemer and revelator.

After the resurrection, Paul says in Philippians 2, God *"exalted Him to the highest place and gave him the name that is above every name, that at the name of Jesus every knee should bow, in heaven and on earth and under the earth, and every tongue confess that Jesus Christ is Lord, to the glory of God the Father" (vs. 9-11).*

The Father Speaks

"Ask of me, and I will make the nations your inheritance, the ends of the earth your possession." But the acknowledgement of that for the sovereigns of the earth should begin now, not later. *"Therefore, you kings, be wise; be warned, you rulers of the earth …" (v 10).* When the Rock of Messiah's kingdom smites the ten toed image, the confederated kingdoms at the end of the age, the whole colossus of man's vaunted power crumbles to the ground, and shall be ground to powder (Matthew 21:44)

Therefore the warning goes out, *"Serve the Lord with fear (awe and reverence) and rejoice with trembling."* Fear and rejoicing are not antagonistic terms. Spurgeon wrote, "Fear without joy is torment; and joy without holy fear would be presumption."

Pay homage to the Son, lest His anger and wrath flare out against you! (v 12). In *The Revelation*, we have the awesome vision of the Wrathful Lamb coming on The Day of the Lord.

> *"Then the kings of the earth, the princes, the generals, the rich, the mighty, and every slave and every free man hid in caves and among the rocks of the mountains and the rocks, 'Fall on us and hide us from the face of him who sits on the throne and from the wrath of the Lamb! For the great day of their wrath has come, and who can stand? (Revelation 6:15-17).*

Paul's summary of this is given in his prologue to Romans, *"The gospel … regarding his Son, who as to his human nature was a descendant of David, and who through the Spirit of holiness was declared with power to be the Son of God by his resurrection from the dead: Jesus Christ our Lord" (Romans 1:1-4).*

> *Sovereign Lord, you are exalted to the place of highest authority and power. You are King of kings and Lord of lords, and before you every knee shall bow, in heaven, on earth, and under the earth, and every tongue will confess that you are Lord to the glory of the Father. In this quiet hour, let my heart gladly submit to your Lordship over every facet*

of my life, time, talent, and treasure. Let me not be guilty of glibly saying, "Lord, Lord …" and fail to do what you direct. Our hearts eagerly anticipate that day of triumph when you reign on David's throne in sovereign majesty, in righteousness, and in justice.

Things To Ponder

1. In the Gospels, the message was *"Repent: for the kingdom of heaven is near."* That message has never been more urgent than now, as nations jockey for power, and Israel is once again the focus of the surrounding nations' wrath. Where will it all end? We know *how* it will end, but not *when*. Let us be watchful. Let us be faithful.

2. *"God laughs at them."* He is actually amused at the arrogance of the nations. He is very much in charge!

Psalm 3

*"Outnumbered
But Not Overwhelmed"*

Psalm 3

1 O Lord, how many are my foes!
  How many rise up against me!

2 Many are saying of me,
  "God will not deliver him. Selah.

3 But you are a shield around me, O Lord;
  you bestow glory on me and lift up my head.

4 To the Lord I cry aloud,
  and he answers me from his holy hill. Selah.

5 I lie down and sleep;
  I wake again, because the Lord sustains me.

6 I will not fear the tens of thousands
  drawn up against me on every side.

7 Arise, O Lord!
  Deliver me, O my God!
  Strike all my enemies on the jaw;
  break the teeth of the wicked.

8 From the Lord comes deliverance.
  May your blessing be on your people. Selah.

NIV

The King's Deliverance*

Psalm 3

A Morning Prayer

"I lie down and sleep; I wake again, because the Lord sustains me" (v 5).

I. The Prediction. *"God **will not deliver** him" (v 2).*

His foes are ...

A. Numerous. *"O Lord, how **many** are my foes!" (v 1)*
B. Dangerous. *"How **many rise up against** me!" (v 1)*
C. Contemptuous. *"**Many are saying** to me, 'God will not deliver him'"*
(v 2).

II. The Petition. *"Arise, O Lord! **Deliver me**, O my God!" (v 7).*

A. **The Lord lifts my head.** *"But you are a shield around me, O Lord, my Glorious One, who lifts up my head" (v 3)*
B. **The Lord hears my cry.** *"To the Lord I cry aloud, and he answers me from His holy hill" (v 4).*
C. **The Lord sustains my life.** *"I lie down and sleep; I wake again, because the Lord sustains me" (v 5).*
D. **The Lord calms my fears.** *"I will not fear the tens of thousands drawn up against me on every side" (v 6).*

III. The Provision. *"From the Lord comes **deliverance**" (v 8).*

A. **The Lord fights for me**. *"For you have struck all my enemies on the jaw; you have broken the teeth of the wicked" (v 7).*
B. **The Lord delivers me.** *"From the Lord comes deliverance."*
"May your blessing be on your people" (v 8).

*The title suggests the possibility that David may have been fleeing from his son, Absalom when he tried to usurp the throne. This adds a note of pathos.

Psalm 3

Outnumbered But Not Overwhelmed

Have you ever come to the place in your life when things just seemed to crowd in on you, nothing seemed to be going right, and the pressure of daily living became almost unbearable?

Here in Psalm 3, David describes for us such an experience of his. One morning he awakened to the sense of being hemmed in on every side by his enemies. This was probably literally true since the heading suggests that he was fleeing from his own son, Absalom, who was trying to wrest the throne from him. Trying to break the spirit and morale of the camp, the taunt had been forwarded from the enemy, *"God will not deliver him."* Nothing or no one is going to spare you this time. You might as well give up! Then in verse 7, David counters with a prayer, *"Arise, O Lord! Deliver me, O my God!"* David wasn't sure of his enemy, but he was sure of his God. And finally, the psalm concludes with the note of assurance in verse 8, *"From the Lord comes deliverance."*

So let's look at the psalm briefly from this threefold perspective, first, the prediction, second, the petition, and finally, the provision.

The Prediction Of The Enemy

David had this sense of the enemy closing in on him. He describes his foes as *numerous. "O Lord, how many are my foes!" (v 1).* Troubles have a way of over-taking us in quantity, don't they? Maybe we could handle a few at a time with a span of time in between trials, but it just seems like trouble so often gangs up on us, and threatens to overwhelm us like the rushing of a mighty wave at high tide. They just outnumber and overpower us sometimes.

David says that they are not only numerous, but they are also *dangerous. "How many rise up against me!"* They have one thing in mind, his defeat and destruction.

And he adds, his foes are *contemptuous. "Many are saying of me, 'God will not deliver him'" (v 2).* Sometimes it seems like God has forsaken us. The enemy of our soul loves to impress us with the number of those who fight with him. A good illustration of this is found in 2 Kings 6:15-17. The king of Syria had surrounded Elisha by night with a host of horses and chariots, intending to capture him in the morning.

"When the servant of the man of God got up and went out early the next morning, an army with horses and chariots had surrounded the city. 'Oh, my lord, what shall we do?' the servant said. 'Don't be afraid,' the prophet answered. 'Those who are with us are more than those who are with them.' And Elisha prayed, 'O Lord, open his eyes so he may see.' Then the Lord opened the servant's eyes, and he looked and saw the hills full of horses and chariots of fire all around Elisha.'"

The apostle Paul talks about a real unseen world that is all around us, and that, he tells us, is where our real warfare goes on. Our fight, he insists, is not with "flesh and blood" enemies, but with unseen powers that continually war against us.

So our enemy tries to impress us with numbers and intimidate us with fear tactics saying that we needn't expect any help from the Lord. There are no words that wound more deeply than those that suggest God has somehow forsaken us. Our enemy loves to create doubt in our mind that God loves us and cares about us. He's been doing that from the very beginning! Remember the disciples on the storm-tossed sea crying out to their Lord, *"Lord, don't you care that we are perishing!"* And one of the enemy's tactics is to insinuate that we don't deserve God's help. And he brings to our remembrance those times when we have failed the Lord and been unfaithful to Him. It may even be a forgiven sin, but the enemy loves to drag it up again, and throw it in our face.

Now what did David do in the face of these intimidations and taunts? He turned to the Lord in prayer.

The Petition To The Lord

He reminds himself of the Lord's faithfulness to him so many times in the past when he was up against a persistent foe. *"You are a shield around me, O Lord, my Glorious One, who lifts up my head" (v 3).* It's good strategy to get your focus off of the enemy and on to the Lord! It takes an effort of the will, but it pays off.

Joshua and Caleb urged the people of Israel to do that as they camped on the banks of the Jordan. They had just gotten back from a reconnaissance of the land. "Your looking at the wrong things," they said, "Get your eyes off of the Jordan, Jericho, and the giants. God is bigger than all of them put together! One plus God is a majority." That, of course, is a loose translation, but it's what they said in essence.

David felt that way. He put the Lord between him and his foes. Long before the psalmist's day, the Lord had said to Abram, *"Fear not, Abram: I am your shield, and your exceeding great reward" (Gen. 15:1).* When we, like David, begin to contemplate the tremendous resources we have in God, the overwhelming pressures seem less overwhelming. He *"lifts up our head."* "We can straighten up, lift our head, raise our hand and go out to meet those foes head on!

Why can the psalmist so readily do this? Because experience has taught him that God hears and answers prayer. *"To the Lord I cry aloud, and he answers me from His holy hill" (v 4).* Many times before he had gone to the Lord. It had become the habit pattern of his life. His feet had been accustomed to treading the road to God's presence, and he can find his way there even in the darkest night.

Because he is confident in the Lord's protection and His answer to his petition, he can go to sleep without fear. The Lord is awake and watching. That is sufficient. And he awakens refreshed and exulting in God's sustaining grace (v 5). All fear is banished. *"I will not fear the tens of thousands drawn up against me on every side" (v 6).* It reminds us of his affirmation elsewhere, *"The Lord is with me; I will not be afraid. What can man do to me? The Lord is with me; he is my helper. I will look in triumph on my enemies" (118: 6, 7).*

The Provision Of The Lord

So the psalm moves from a taunt that God will not deliver, to a prayer asking for His deliverance, to the provision of deliverance! David is assured that the Lord will fight his battle for him. *"You have struck all my enemies on the jaw; you have broken the teeth of the wicked" (v 7).* The Lord will fight for me! The Lord will deliver me!

Such are the assurances that fill David's heart. The enemy is still there, but the victory seems assured.

His final petition is that the Lord might bless His people even as he himself had been the recipient of the Lord's blessing.

He was outnumbered but not overcome!

Why not try David's approach to overwhelming circumstances?

Heavenly Father, at times I do feel overcome, overwhelmed. Things press in, trouble seems to come in triplicate, and there doesn't seem to be any way out. Yet, I am comforted to remember, along with David, that you specialize in deliverance. Nothing is too hard for you! With you as my rescuer, my foes cannot win.

Things to Ponder

The great redemptive program outlined in Scripture is God's "rescue mission." We were lost; God found us. We were sick; God healed us. We were sinking in sin; God lifted us up out of the miry pit and set us on a rock! Indeed, He specializes in deliverance. Praise His name!

Psalm 4

"How To Get A Good Night's Sleep"

Psalm 4

For the director of music.
With stringed instruments.

A psalm of David.

1 Answer me when I call to you, O my righteous God.
    Give me relief from my distress;
    be merciful to me and hear my prayer.

2 How long, O men, will you turn my glory into shame?
    How long will you love delusions and seek false gods? Selah

3 Know that the LORD has set apart the godly for himself;
    the LORD will hear when I call to him.

4 In your anger do not sin; when you are on your beds,
    search your hearts and be silent. Selah

5 Offer right sacrifices and trust in the LORD.

6 Many are asking, "Who can show us any good?"
    Let the light of your face shine upon us, O LORD.

7 You have filled my heart with greater joy
    than when their grain and new wine abound.

8 I will lie down and sleep in peace,
    for you alone, O LORD, make me dwell in safety.

NIV

Psalm 4

How To Get A Good Night's Sleep

"I will lie down and sleep, for you alone, O Lord, make me dwell in safety"
(Psalm 4:8).

Just before you close your eyes in sleep, there are three things you might do
with profit that are suggested here by the psalmist:

I. Request.

Four urgent requests are made:

A. Answer me
B. Give relief to me
C. Be merciful to me
D. Hear me (v 1)

The Lord opposes the **proud.** *"men "[you sons of the great]*
The Lord honors the **humble** *"the godly," [the man of kindness) (v 2)*

II. Reflect.

A. On your attitude toward others. *"In your anger do not sin" (vs. 4)*
Note Ephesians 4:6 *"… do not let the sun go down while you are still
angry"*
B. On the quality of your own thoughts. *"search your hearts" (v 4)* See
Psalm 139:23.
C. On your relationship to God. *"Be silent …" "be still and know that I
am God." "Offer sacrifices that are righteous …"* (See Psalm 51:16-19)
"Trust in the Lord" (v 4-5).

III. Rejoice.

    A. His detractors say, *"Who can show us any good?" (Vs. 6)*
    B. The psalmist knows His Lord is good.

        1. His love *"Let the light of your face shine upon us, O Lord" (v 6)*
        2. His joy *"You have filled my heart with greater joy than when their grain and new wine abound" (v 7)*
        3. His peace *"I will lie down and sleep in peace, for you alone, O Lord, make me dwell in safety" (v 8)*

Psalm 4

How To Get A Good Night's Sleep

We have seen that Psalm 3 is a morning prayer. Psalm 4 is an evening prayer. David has come to the end of the day and is able to say, *"I will lie down and sleep in peace, for you alone, O Lord, make me dwell in safety" (v 8)*. Note that the language is similar, *"I lie down and sleep,"* he says in chapter 3 and verse 5, and here he says, *"I will lie down and sleep ..."* There are also two challenges by the enemy to his faith. *"Many are saying to me ..." (3:2)*, and here, *"Many are asking ..." (4:6)*. The one questions his *security* and the other his *prosperity*. The first says, "You won't receive any help!" and the second says, "You won't receive any good!"

The palmist knows better. He is not perturbed. He does not allow the enemy to disquiet him or disturb him.

And herein is a wonderful lesson for each of us: If your confidence and trust is in the Lord, nothing can ruffle your composure. Someone has said, "The rest of your life depends on the rest of your nights." Many people, though, feel like the little boy who was having trouble falling asleep. He told his mother, "My body is lying down, but my mind keeps sitting up!"

If anxious thoughts keep you awake, ask the Lord to quiet your heart and give you the faith to be able to relax and let Him solve the problems that disturb you.

Just before you close your eye in sleep, and while you lay in your bed quietly, there are three things you might do with profit that are suggested here by the psalmist, David.

First, it is a good time for *requesting*, second, a good time for *reflecting*, and finally, a good time for *rejoicing*.

Request

In other words, take a few moments to commit your day and your way to the Lord. Psalm 4 begins with prayer. Four urgent requests are made:

> *Answer me*
>> *Give relief to me*
>>> *Be merciful to me*
>>>> *Hear me*

And notice that God is addressed as *"O my righteous God".* He is saying that God doesn't make mistakes; that His ways are right and good and appropriate.

The next two verses seem to be somewhat unrelated to the opening prayer, but I would like to suggest a relationship. In verses 2 and 3, he stresses the kind of person, first, that God *opposes,* and second, the kind of person he *honors.* When we approach the Lord, there is an attitude that we are to have that assures that the Lord will hear us when we call on him (v 3b). Peter in His first epistle gives us the principle of God's operation, *"God opposes the proud but gives grace to the humble."* So the psalmist here suggests that God opposes the haughty. The phrase, *"How long, O men …"* could be translated, *"You sons of the great!"*

These who consider themselves great are characterized in a threefold way …

> You hate righteousness
> > You love emptiness
> > > You seek falsehood

In their pride, they set themselves against God and His way, and opt for a path of shame and sham.

On the other hand, in verse 3, the psalmist mentions the kind of person God delights to honor—the humble. *"Know that the Lord has set apart the godly-'the man of kindness'-for himself."* This is the kind of person whose heart is open and sensitive to the Lord, and delights to reflect his actions and attitudes in the world.

Peter concludes his statement in I Peter 5 by saying, *"Humble yourselves, therefore, under God's mighty hand, that He may lift you up in due time. Cast your anxiety on Him because He cares for you."* (5:6, 7)

On our bed, before sleep overtakes us, it is a good time for requesting, just committing our day and our way to Him. But it is also a good time for reflecting.

Reflect.

"In your anger do not sin; when you are on your beds, search your hearts and be silent. Offer right sacrifices and trust in the Lord." (v 4 and 5)

First, it is a good time to reflect on *your attitude toward others. "In your anger do not sin."* Paul quotes this in Ephesians 4 and verse 6, and adds a clarifying thought, *"In your anger do not sin: do not let the sun go down while you are still angry."* In this time of reflecting just before sleep overtakes you, you may remember that you have something against another or someone has something against you. You may have been guilty of harsh words or inappropriate attitudes or actions toward that spouse, that child, or that friend. Confess these things to the Lord, and let him dissolve the bitterness in your heart and dissipate the poison of resentment from your soul.

Second, he suggests that this time of reflection could be *an opportunity for searching your own heart*. *"Reflect in your heart … search your heart."* The psalmist expands on that in Psalm 139:23, *"Search me, O God, and know my heart; test me and know my anxious thoughts. See if there is any offensive way in me, and lead me in the way everlasting."*

Third, as you reflect, it could be a time to *examine your relationship to God*. *"Be silent … be still and know that I am God. Offer sacrifices that are righteous."* What does he mean by that? Well he explains it in Psalm 51 verses 1:6-18: *"You do not delight in sacrifice, or I would bring it; you do not take pleasure in burnt offering. The sacrifices of God are a broken and contrite heart. 0, God, you will not despise."* And then he adds, *"Then there will be righteous sacrifices …" (v 19)*

So there is an outward, inward, and upward look that can take place. He concludes this section by saying, *"Trust in the Lord."* So many of our problems would be simplified if we could only learn to put our confidence and trust and dependence in the Lord!

Finally, as we lie quietly on our bed, first requesting and then reflecting, let this conclude with rejoicing.

Rejoice.

His detractors chide him, *"Who can show us any good"* or *"Who will let us see prosperity?"* And his testimony is that the Lord, when He smiles His approval upon his own, grants them abundant goodness and gladness. *"Let the light of your face shine upon us, O Lord. You have filled my heart with greater joy than when their grain and new wine abound."*

And so rehearse the goodness of the Lord and let him fill your heart with great rejoicing! What a great way to end the day!

Thus by this simple process of requesting, reflecting, and rejoicing, the psalmist closes his day. He is still experiencing stress. He is hemmed in from all sides. His enemies still taunt him. But his heart is at rest. *"I will lie down and sleep in peace, for you alone, O Lord, make me dwell in safety."*

During the last great war an elderly woman in England had endured the nerve-wracking bombings with amazing serenity. When asked to give the secret of her calmness amid the terror and danger, she replied, "Well, every night I say my prayers. And then I remember that God is always watching, so I go peacefully to sleep. After all, there is no need for both of us to stay awake!"

Before you sleep, just gently lay
Every troubled thought away;
Drop your burden and your care
In the quiet arms of prayer. Anonymous.

Father, help me to pause before slipping off into sleep, to reflect on the day and use these quiet moments to allow the Spirit to speak whatever message He might wish to give. Let no sin remain unconfessed, no disquieting thought to trouble my restfulness. Grant your peace. Amen.

Thoughts To Ponder

"You alone, O Lord, make me dwell in safety." Reflect on Fanny Crosby's great hymn,

Safe in the arms of Jesus,
Safe from corroding care,
Safe from the world's temptations,
Sin cannot harm me there.
Free from the blight of sorrow,
Free from my doubts and fears;
Only a few more trials,
Only a few more tears.
Safe in the arms of Jesus,
Safe on His gentle breast,
There by His love o'ershaded,
Sweetly my soul shall rest.

Psalm 5

"By God's Great Mercy"

Psalm 5

For the director of music.
For flutes.
A psalm of David.

1 Give ear to my words, O LORD, consider my sighing.
2 Listen to my cry for help, my King and my God,
    for to you I pray.
3 In the morning, O LORD, you hear my voice;
    in the morning I lay my requests before you and wait in expectation.

4 You are not a God who takes pleasure in evil;
    with you the wicked cannot dwell.
5 The arrogant cannot stand in your presence;
    you hate all who do wrong.
6 You destroy those who tell lies;
    bloodthirsty and deceitful men the LORD abhors.

7 But I, by your great mercy, will come into your house;
    in reverence will I bow down toward your holy temple.
8 Lead me, O LORD in your righteousness
    because of my enemies make straight your way before me.

9 Not a word from their mouth can be trusted;
    their heart is filled with destruction.
    their throat is an open grave;
    with their tongue they speak deceit.
10 Declare them guilty, O God!
    Let their intrigues be their downfall.
Banish them for their many sins,
    for they have rebelled against you.

11 But let all who take refuge in you be glad;
    let them ever sing for joy.
    Spread your protection over them,
    that those who love your name may rejoice in you.

12 For surely, O LORD, you bless the righteous;
    you surround them with your favor as with a shield.

NIV

Psalm 5

By Your Great Mercy

*"But I, **by your great mercy**, will come into your house; in reverence will I bow down toward your holy temple" (5:7).*

I. The Prayer. Personal and Passionate.

    A. He comes earnestly.

        1. Speaking *"Give ear to **my words**, Lord"*
        2. Sighing *"Consider **my sighing***
        3. Crying *"Listen to **my cry** for help, my King and my God, for to you I pray" (vs. 1, 2).*

    B. He comes early. *"**In the morning**, O Lord, in the morning" (v 3).*
    C. He comes expectantly. *"I lay my requests before you and wait **in expectation**" (v 3)*

II. The Audition. Who Can Come Into God's Presence?

    A. The Wicked Cannot Come.

        1. God is displeased with evil. *"You are not a God who takes pleasure in evil; with you the wicked cannot dwell"*
        2. God rejects the proud *"The arrogant cannot stand in your presence"*
        3. God hates wrong doers *"you hate all who do wrong"*
        4. God destroys liars *"You destroy those who tell lies"*
        5.God abhors the violent and deceitful. *"bloodthirsty and deceitful men the Lord abhors" (v 4-6).*

B. The Righteous May Come.

1. With the proper awareness. *"But I, by your great mercy, will come ..."*
2. In the proper attitude.

+ Reverently *"in reverence will I bow down ..."*
+ Dependently *"Lead me, O Lord, in your righteousness because of my enemies"*
+ Obediently *".... make straight your way before me" (v 8).*

III. The Argument. Why the Wicked Are Rejected and the Righteous Blessed?

A. The Wicked Rejected.

1. They are recognized for what they are:

+ Their mouth—dishonest
+ Their heart—destructive
+ Their throat—corruptive
+ Their tongue—deceptive

2. They are rejected for what they do.

+ Their intrigues. *"Let their intrigues be their downfall"*
+ Their sin *"Banish them for their many sins, for ..."*
+ Their rebellion *"... they have rebelled against you" (v 10)*

B. The Righteous Blessed. *"For surely, O Lord, you bless the righteous"*

1. They are joyful. *"But let all who take refuge in you be glad; let them ever sing for joy"*
2. They are protected *"Spread your protection over them, that those who love your name may rejoice in you" (v 11).*
3. They are favored *"you surround them with your favor as with a shield" (v 1 2).*

Note: The Lord is my King (v 2)
    The Lord is my God (v 2)
        The Lord is my Shepherd (v 8)
            The Lord is my Song (v 11)
                The Lord is my Shield (v 12)

Psalm 5

By Your Great Mercy

David wrote and delivered this psalm to the choir director to be sung and accompanied by flutes. Wouldn't you like to have heard it sung in the temple worship? It is a morning psalm, and stresses the typical contrast between the righteous and the wicked begun in the introductory psalm, Psalm 1. We first focus on the prayer of the psalmist that is both personal and passionate.

The Prayer

Personal

The *personal* aspect of the psalm is highlighted by the pronoun *"my"*. No one can stand in for us at the throne.

Passionate

The *passionate* nature of his prayer is seen in the progression *"my words,"* *"my sighing,"* and *"my cry"*. As he prays, it is seen that the psalmist comes to God first of all *earnestly*. Words deepen into sighs and rise to a cry. The apostle reminds us in Romans 8 that sometimes when we cannot find the words, *"the Spirit himself intercedes for us with groans that words cannot express. And he who searches our hearts knows the mind of the Spirit, because the Spirit intercedes for the saints in accordance with God's will"* (v. 27-28).

The prayer is also offered *early*. *"In the morning, O Lord, in the morning"* (v 3). Prayer is always a good springboard to launch the day.

Then note also, that the psalmist comes *expectantly*. *"I lay my requests before you and wait in expectation"* (v 3). The psalmist actually says, *"I set in order ..."* much as a priest does as he prepares the morning sacrifice. And then he *"looks up"* expectantly anticipating the answer to come. This is the only way to pray, confident that God hears and will answer, and we must be alert to recognize the answer when it comes.

I am reminded of a story I read once about the Yorkshire class leader, Daniel Quorum. He was visiting with one of his friends, and said,

"I am sorry you have met with such a great disappointment."

"Why no," said his friend, "I have not met with any disappointment."

"Yes," said Daniel, "you were expecting something remarkable today."

"What do you mean?"

"Why, you prayed that you might be kept sweet and gentle all day long. And, by the way things have been going, I see you have been greatly disappointed!" God never disappoints those who come to Him believing and expecting that He will answer.

Next, the psalmist emphasizes those who can get an audition with God, those who can come into His presence.

The Audition

It was Spurgeon who said, "Rest assured, Christ will not live in the parlor of our hearts if we entertain the devil in the cellar of our thoughts."

The Wicked Cannot Come

Certainly, *the wicked cannot come* into God's presence. And the reasons are marshaled.

First, He says that God is **displeased with evil.** *"You are not a God who takes pleasure in evil; with you the wicked cannot dwell" (v 4)* Elsewhere it is stated *"if I regard iniquity in my heart, the Lord will not hear me."* He reminds us again that God is a holy God.

Second, God **rejects the proud.** *"The arrogant cannot stand in your presence" (v 5).* Peter underscores this in his first epistle, chapter 5 where he quotes Proverbs 3:34, *"God opposes the proud but gives grace to the humble."* Then he continues by admonishing his readers, *"Humble yourselves, therefore, under God's mighty hand, that he may lift you up in due time" (v 6).*

In the third place, he tells us that God **hates wrong doers.** *"You hate all who do wrong" (v 5).* It may seem sometimes that those who do wrong get away with it, but *"God is not mocked. Whatever a man sows he reaps."* If wrong seed is sown, the harvest will be sure. *"Sow the wind and reap the whirlwind."*

Again we are told that God **destroys liars.** *"You destroy those who tell lies" (v 6).* In Revelation 21, liars are included along with *"the cowardly, the unbelieving, the vile, the murderers, the sexually immoral, those who practice magic arts ..."* as those whose destination is the lake of fire, the second death (v 8).

And finally, it is stated that **God abhors (strong word) the violent and deceitful.** *"... the bloodthirsty and deceitful men the Lord abhors" (v. 6).* It is little wonder that wicked men cannot approach a holy God.

The Righteous May Come

In verse 7, there is a definite contrast intended by the words *"But I, by your great mercy will come …"* Thus the psalmist contrasts himself with the wicked. But he comes not because he is worthy to come, but because of God's great love for him.

His Awareness

That is his *awareness*, and it most certainly should be ours. We are permitted to come into God's holy presence, not because we are somehow deserving of such a privilege, but because in His grace and mercy, God has provided the means of access to Himself through the shed blood of the appointed sacrifice- His beloved Son. Hebrews 10 shows the way, *"Therefore, brothers, since we have confidence to enter the Most Holy Place by the blood of Jesus, by a new and living way opened for us through the curtain, that is, his body …" (v 19-20).*

His Attitude

Likewise, there is an *attitude* that goes along with the awareness. How does the psalmist come? First, he comes *reverently*. *"In reverence will I bow down."* In the second place, he comes *dependently*. He wants his enemies to know that his confidence is in His God who leads him continuously in the right way, directing him and protecting him. *"Lead me, O Lord, in your righteousness because of my enemies" (v 8).* It follows, then, that he comes to God *obediently*. He wants God to *"make straight his way" (v 8).* Knowing the way of righteousness, it is his desire to walk in that way.

Finally, David offers a further argument as to why the wicked are rejected by God and the righteous are blessed.

The Argument.

The Wicked Are Rejected

The wicked are *rejected*. They are recognized for **what they are**: There mouth is *dishonest*. *"Not a word in their mouth can be trusted" (v 9).* One cannot bank on anything they say. Their heart is *destructive*. *"Their heart is filled with destruction" (v 9).* They mean to hurt and harm rather than offer anything constructive. Their throat he likens to an open grave. The *corruptive* power of the grave is probably here in view. Talk about halitosis! And finally, from their mouth comes words calculated to deceive. They are *deceptive.*

And what they are is augmented by **what they do.** David prays that they might be declared guilty, which, of course, is the opposite of being justified to God. He mentions *"their intrigues," "their sins,"* and *"their rebellion"* as reasons for condemnation.

The Righteous Are Blessed

And again we have the *"but". "But let all who take refuge in you be glad ..."*

The righteous, by contrast, are **blessed.** *"For surely, O Lord, you bless the righteous."(v 12).* And being blessed, they are also **joyful.** *"... those who love your name ... rejoice in you" (v 11)* Still further, they are *protected. "Spread your protection over them" (v 11).* And finally, they are *favored. "You surround them with your favor as with a shield" (v 12).*

Going back, then, we see that the wicked leave themselves vulnerable to the judgment of God, while the righteous are personally loved and accepted by God. David makes it very personal:

The Lord is my King (v 2)
   The Lord is my God (v 2)
      The Lord is my Shepherd (v 8)
         The Lord is my Song (v 11)
            The Lord is my Shield (v 12)
And all this is because of His great mercy and love!

Father, it is such a priceless privilege we have of being your children, and being able to call you 'Father,' and having direct access, coming boldly to your throne. Jesus, Thy dear Son and our Savior, made the way open for us through the rent veil of His flesh. Approaching your throne of grace with confidence, we "find grace to help us in our time of need."

Something To Ponder

A 'new and living way' has been opened for us into the holy of holies (Heb. 10:20). And since we have a Great High Priest in heaven that is our Advocate, we are admonished

1. To draw near to God with a sincere heart and full assurance of **faith.**

2. To hold unswervingly to the **hope** we profess.

3. To consider how we may spur one another on toward **love** and good deeds.

Faith, hope and love are our "response-ability", our ability to respond to God's grace and mercy. Are we availing ourselves of this marvelous privilege of prayer early and often?

Psalm 6

"How Long, O Lord?"

Psalm 6

For the director of music.
With stringed instruments
According to sheminith.

A Psalm of David

1 O Lord, do not rebuke me in your anger
    or discipline me in your wrath.
2 Be merciful to me, Lord, for I am faint;
    O Lord, heal me, for my bones are in agony.
3 My soul is in anguish.
    How long, O Lord, how long?

4 Turn, O Lord, and deliver me;
    save me because of your unfailing love.
5 No one remembers you when he is dead.
    Who praise you from the grave?

6 I am worn out from groaning,
    all night long I flood my bed with weeping
    and drench my couch with tears.
7 My eyes grow weak with sorrow;
    they fail because of all my foes.

8 Away from me, all you who do evil,
    for the Lord has heard my weeping.
9 The Lord has heard my cry for mercy;
    the Lord accepts my prayer.
10 All my enemies will be ashamed and dismayed;
    they will turn back in sudden disgrace.

NIV

Psalm 6

How Long, O Lord?

A Psalm of David

"How long, O Lord, how long?" (v 3)

I. His Desperation.

A. He feels condemnation. *"O Lord, do not rebuke me in your anger or discipline me in your wrath" (v 1)*
B. He feels desperation. *"I am faint … my bones are in agony. My soul is in anguish" (v*
C. He feels depression. *"I am worn out from groaning; all night long I flood my bed with weeping, and drench my couch with tears. My eyes grow weak with sorrow, they fail." (v 6-7).*
D. He feels oppression." *… because of all my foes" (v 7) "all who do evil" (v 8) "all my enemies" (v 10).*

II. His Supplication.

A. Be merciful to me. *"Be merciful to me, Lord," (v. 2)*
B. Heal me. *"O Lord, heal me," (v. 2)*
C. Turn and deliver me. *"Turn, O Lord, and deliver me …" (v 4)*
D. Save me … because of your unfailing love. *"Save me because of your unfailing love" (v 4)*

III. His Confirmation.

A. The Lord is mindful of his distress. *"… the Lord has heard my weeping" (v 8)*
B. The Lord accepts his prayer. *"The Lord has heard my cry for mercy; the Lord accepts my prayer" (v 9)*
C. The Lord will deal with his enemies—they will be …

1. Dispersed *"Away from me, all you who do evil"* (v 8)
2. Ashamed *"All my enemies will be ashamed ..."* (v. 10
3. Dismayed *"... and dismayed"* (v 10)
4. Disgraced *"they will turn back in sudden disgrace"* (v 10).

Father, the psalmist cries "Save me" and then offers the reason, "because of your unfailing love." I contemplate that 'unfailing love" and am reminded that it was supremely demonstrated when you gave your One and Only Son to die for us even when we were enemies.

Psalm 6

How Long, O Lord?

This psalm is what is called a Penitential Psalm. It is the first of seven great penitential psalms that are recorded for us. David realized full well that God permitted Absalom's rebellion as a penal consequence of his sin. Here it is more the effect of what sin has wrought than the sin itself that is in view. He knows that sin must be punished, and he is overwhelmed by a sense of guilt and cries out in desperation for divine clemency.

His Desperation.

First, he feels **condemnation.** *"O Lord, do not rebuke me in your anger or discipline me in your wrath" (v 1).* David knows that with God there is the chastisement of anger and the chastisement of grace. The one is overwhelming and the other is measured; the one destroys and the other perfects. He pleads for God's chastisement to be in love not in anger.

Then, in the second place, he feels **desperation.** *"I am faint … my bones are in agony. My soul is in anguish" (vv 2-3).* Spurgeon said, "Soul-trouble is the very soul of trouble." The physical affects the spiritual and vice-versa. He appeals to God's mercy, his unfailing love, for deliverance (v 4). He tells God that if his punishment is a death-sentence, there will be one less voice among the living to praise Him. *"No one remembers you when he is dead. Who praises you from the grave?" (v 5).*

Next, he feels deep **depression.** *"I am worn out from groaning; all night long I flood my bed with weeping, and drench my couch with tears. My eyes grow weak with sorrow; they fail …" (v 6-7).* This whole business had really gotten him down. He was, so to speak, "in the pits".

And it is obvious, that he also has a sense of **oppression** caused by his enemies besetting him on every side. *"… because of all my foes" (v 7).* "all who do evil" (v 8), "all my enemies" (v 10). If God would be so gracious to deliver him from his sin, perhaps his grace would extend to deliverance over his enemies.

David, in the midst of his sense of desperation, cried out to God, His only Hope and Savior.

His Supplication.

He cries for the Lord to be merciful to him, to heal him, to turn (return) and deliver him, and to save him *"because of your unfailing love."* In his darkness, David feels the absence of God, and pleads for him to return and restore him. He pleads, *"How long, O Lord?"* (See 13:1; 74:9f) He longs for a ray of light to penetrate the darkness he feels. Many an anguished, depressed soul has felt his pain.

Then the light begins to break!

His Confirmation.

Suddenly his countenance brightens. He senses that the Lord is mindful of his distress. *"The*
Lord has heard my weeping" (v 8). The Lord had been there all along, listening, waiting. What a comfort the psalmist feels! He had prayed for mercy. The answer now comes with a sense of great relief, *"The Lord has heard my cry for mercy; the Lord accepts my prayer" (v 9)*. The Scriptures say that our God is *"rich in mercy"*. Indeed He is! Someone has said grace is getting from God what we don't deserve, and mercy is not getting from God what we do deserve.

And he is confident that the Lord would deal with his enemies also. They will be dispersed, ashamed, dismayed, and disgraced. *"Away from me (depart from me), all you who do evil … all my enemies will be ashamed and dismayed; they will turn back in sudden disgrace" (v 8, 10)*.

If you are in "between a rock and a hard place," this psalm is for you. God does not turn a deaf ear to the penitent heart that cries out in anguish for His grace and mercy.

It is said that St. Augustine, in his last sickness, ordered these penitential psalms to be inscribed in a visible place on a wall of his chamber, where he might fix his eyes and heart upon them, and make their words his own in the breathing out of his soul to God.

Yet, as a redeemed child of God, I remind myself that God has offered to me a full and complete forgiveness because of Christ. I rejoice in those verses that tell me there is now no condemnation. Hear our Lord's word in John 3:17, *"For God did not send his Son into the world to condemn the world, but to save the world through him."* And this because of His great love and mercy! Or remember Paul's great word in Romans 8:34, *"Who is he that condemns? Christ Jesus, who died— more than that, who was raised to life—is at the right hand of God and is also interceding for us."* Yes, and I could martial many more. Certainly we should mourn for our sin that made it necessary for Christ to die in order to bear them away. But, thank God, He did bear them, and took them away—forever.

Lord, I fall at your feet as the adulterous woman did, and hear from your lips the question, "Does no one condemn you?" And I believe I can confidently say, "No one, Lord." Your reply comes to me as a healing balm, "Neither do I condemn you. Go and sin no more." The apostle asks a similar question, "Who is he that condemns?" Then answers his own question: "Christ Jesus, who died—more than that, who was raised to life—is at the right hand of God and is also interceding for us." Blessed assurance!

> Blessed assurance, Jesus is mine!
> O what a foretaste of glory divine!
> Heir of salvation, purchase of God,
> Born of His Spirit, washed in His blood.
>
> —Fanny Crosby

Things To Ponder

All who are familiar with Paul's great treatise in Romans 8 know it begins with 'no condemnation' and ends with 'no separation.' The apostle asks five questions, and answers them …

> Any opposition?
> Any limitation?
> Any accusation?
> Any condemnation?
> Any separation?

The answer to each is a resounding 'No!' And all because of Jesus!

Psalm 7

"The Slandered Soul"

Psalm 7

A shiggaion of David,
That he sang to the LORD concerning Cush, a Benjamite.

1 O LORD my God, I take refuge in you;
      save and deliver me from all who pursue me,
2 or they will tear me like a lion and rip me
      to pieces with no one to rescue me.

3 O LORD my God, if I have done this and
      there is guilt on my hands—
4 if I have done evil to him who is at peace
      with me or without cause have robbed my foe—
5 then let my enemy pursue and overtake me;
      let him trample my life to the ground
      and make me sleep in the dust. Selah

6 Arise, O LORD, in your anger;
      rise up against the rage of my enemies.
Awake, my God; decree justice.
7 Let the assembled peoples gather around you.
      Rule over them from on high;
8 let the LORD judge the peoples.
      Judge me, O LORD, according to my righteousness,
      according to my integrity, O Most High.

9 O righteous God, who searches minds and hearts,
      bring to an end the violence of the
      wicked and make the righteous secure.
10 My shield is God Most High,
      who saves the upright in heart.
11 God is a righteous judge, a God who
      expresses his wrath every day.
12 If he does not relent, he will sharpen his sword;
      he will bend and string his bow.

13 He has prepared his deadly weapons;
>   he makes ready his flaming arrows.
14 He who is pregnant with evil
>   and conceives trouble gives birth to disillusionment.

15 He who digs a hole and scoops it out
>   falls into the pit he has made.
16 The trouble he causes recoils on himself;
>   his violence comes down on his own head.
17 I will give thanks to the LORD because of his righteousness
>   and will sing praise to the name of the LORD Most High.

NIV

Psalm 7

The Slandered Soul

A Shiggaion (a disordered, erratic song) of David

I. The Accusation.

A. The accused

> 1. No where to turn but to the Lord "*O LORD my God, I take refuge in you; save and deliver me …*"
> 2. His enemies are intent on his destruction "*they will tear me like a lion and rip me to pieces with no one to rescue me*" (*v 1, 2*).

B. The accusation. He violated the law of *talio* (*lex talionis*=render good for good; evil for evil)

> 1. His accuser's view: he had rendered evil for good, disloyal to his protector; treasonable activity (had bit the hand that fed him)
> 2. David's view: he had rendered good for evil, twice delivered his enemy who had wronged him

C. The disclaimer. If I'm guilty as accused, then I deserve everything I get. "*If I have done this and there is guilt on my hands … if I have done evil … then let my enemies pursue and overtake me; let them trample my life to the ground and make me sleep in the dust. Selah*" (*v 5*).

II. The Appeal For Justice. "*Arise, O LORD, in your anger; rise up against the rage of my enemies. Awake, my God decree justice*" (*v. 6*).

> **A. Assemble the people before your tribunal.** "*Let the assembled people gather around you. Rule over them from on high*" (*v 7*).
> **B. Adjudicate the matter.** "*… let the Lord judge the peoples … judge me …*" (*v 8*)
> **C. Judge righteously** "*O righteous God, who searches minds and hearts …*"

He knows not only what we have done, but why we did it. *"Everything is uncovered and laid bare before the eyes of him to whom we must give account" (Heb. 4:13).*

III. The Adjudication.

A. In favor of the righteous.

1. The verdict sought. *"... bring to an end the violence of the wicked and make the righteous secure" (v 9).*
2. The verdict secured. *"My shield is God Most High, who saves the upright in heart" (v 9, 10).*

B. Against the wicked.

1. The wrath of God is slow, but it is sure. *"God is a righteous judge, a God who expresses his wrath every day" (v 11).* [Gives daily warnings of his displeasure, and of the gathering storm of his wrath.]
2. If the sinner does not repent, God will not relent. *"If he does not relent, he will sharpen his sword; he will bend and string his bow. He has prepared his deadly weapons; he makes ready his flaming arrows" (v 12, 13).*
3. Wickedness is self-defeating. God can surely defeat the wicked, but in most cases they defeat themselves. *"He who is pregnant with evil and conceives trouble gives birth to disillusionment. He who digs a hole and scoops it out falls into the pit he has made. The trouble he causes recoils on himself; his violence comes down on his own head" (v 14-16).*

Concluding Praise. The psalm begins with a sigh, and ends with song!

"I will give thanks to the LORD because of his righteousness and will sing praise to the name of the LORD Most High" (v 17).

Psalm 7

The Slandered Soul

Psalm 7 is the song of a slandered soul. We cannot be absolutely certain, but it appears that Cush the Benjamite had accused David of treasonable activity against King Saul, who was ready to credit it because of his insane jealousy.

Lies against a person's character or actions are very destructive, because they destroy reputations and relationships. In Shakespeare's play Othello, the character Iago describes how damaging slander can be.

> Who steals my purse steals trash;
>   'tis something, nothing.
> 'Twas mine, 'tis his,
>   and has been slave to thousands.
> But he who filches from me my good name
>   robs me of that which not enriches him
> And makes me poor indeed.

Solomon describes slander as verbal arson. *"An ungodly man digs up evil, and it is on his lips like a burning fire" (Proverbs 16:27).* He also said that a person who spreads slander is a fool (Proverbs 10:18).

David had this sense that his enemies were out to destroy him, no matter what it took. It was all the more galling, because he knew that there was not a shred of truth in their accusations.

Let's try to determine first, if we can, what the accusation was. Let me suggest the following.

The Accusation.

David, the accused, cries out to the Lord, from whom he seeks deliverance from his accusers. He really has nowhere he can turn, for no one is willing to stand up for him. *"O Lord my God, I take refuge in you; save and deliver me ..."* He tells the Lord that his enemies are bent on his destruction. *"... they will tear me like a lion and rip me to pieces with no one to rescue me" (v 1, 2).* He speaks very personally, *"Yahweh my God."* He needs to know that his God will champion his cause.

It is not easy to discern the exact nature of the accusation, but some have thought, and I think with good warrant, that they accuse David of violating the *law of talio* or in the Latin, *lex talionis*, which stated that good must be rendered for good, and evil for evil. His accuser's view was that he had broken this law by rendering evil for good. He had been disloyal to his protector and thus his actions were treasonable. They accused him of "biting the hand that fed him." David, in reality, had rendered good for evil, twice delivering his enemy, Saul, who had wronged him. He insisted that he could not touch God's anointed.

And so he offers a strong disclaimer. In effect, he was saying, "If I'm guilty as charged, then I deserve everything I get." *"If I have done this and there is guilt on my hands ... if I have done evil ... then let my enemies pursue and overtake me; let them trample my life to the ground and make me sleep in the dust. Selah" (v 5).* He is not saying that he never does anything wrong, but that in "this" instance, he is without fault.

So he appeals to God for justice.

The Appeal For Justice.

David's appeal seems to imply sleep and inactivity on God's part. *"Arise ... rise up ... awake!"* He needs to see some action by God; his need is urgent and immediate. How like all of us in our impatience. It just seems like God is standing still ... or slumbering. Let the people be assembled before your tribunal! Adjudicate the matter! Judge the people ... judge me! We await your verdict!

David is assured that God will judge righteously. And the reason is that He knows not only what we do but also why we do it. He does not merely judge on the surface of things, but knows even the hidden motives of men's hearts. *"O righteous God, who searches minds and hearts" (v 9).* The author of Hebrews reminds us of the same thing, *"Everything is uncovered and laid bare before the eyes of him to whom we must give account" (Heb. 4:13).*

God is the only one with the credentials to judge. Man makes a poor judge, because he judges only what he can see. There is always one fact more of which he is unaware. And David is confident that if God looks on his heart he will see that he is a man of integrity and had done what was right. His heart did not condemn him even though his accusers did.

He awaits the verdict.

The Adjudication.

God rules *in favor of the righteous*. The verdict that was sought is seen in verse 9, *"... bring to an end the violence of the wicked and make the righteous secure."* That's what all God's people want. They want to see the wicked brought up short, and the righteous delivered from their ceaseless attacks.

And the verdict secured was welcomed indeed. *"My shield is God Most High, who saves the upright in heart" (v 10).*

And God rules *against the wicked*. Verse 11 probably means that the wrath of God is slow, but it is always sure. His attitude toward sin never changes. Every day he gives fresh warnings of his displeasure, and of the gathering storm of his wrath outpoured. *"God is a righteous judge, a God who expresses his wrath every day."* The Book of Revelation reveals that in "the last day" God's wrath will be poured out on a rebellious, unbelieving world that his been given repeated warnings to repent. In the meantime, He is patient *"not willing that any should perish, but that all should come to repentance."*

And if the sinner does not repent, God will not relent. If He relents, all is well; if he does not relent, all is lost. *"If he does not relent, he will sharpen his sword; he will bend and string his bow, he has prepared his deadly weapons; he makes ready his flaming arrow" (v 12, 13).* Turn or burn is the sinner's only alternative.

God can surely defeat the wicked, but in most cases, they defeat themselves. Wickedness is always self-defeating. Sin has a boomerang effect as evidenced by Haman, in Esther day, being hanged on the gallows he had built for Mordecai. *"He who is pregnant with evil and conceives trouble gives birth to disillusionment. He who digs a hole (a snare or trap) and scoops it out falls into the pit he has made. The trouble he causes recoils on himself; his violence comes down on his own head" (v 14-16).* God is not mocked. What a man sows, he will reap.

David feels vindicated, and lifts his voice to praise the LORD. He who had begun with a sigh, now ends with a song!

"I will give thanks to the LORD because of his righteousness and will sing praise to the name of the LORD Most High" (v 17).

> *Lord, it is a sobering thought that you know everything there is to know about us. You know the worst about us, and the best about us, and most of all, what you want to accomplish in us. It is foolish for us to try to cover up our sin from your all-seeing gaze. Rather, you want us to acknowledge it, confess it, for in the Lord Jesus you have provided full forgiveness for all sin for all time—and my sin at this time! Thank you that you are "faithful and just to forgive us and to cleanse us from all unrighteousness!"*

Things To Ponder

Having made sure that we are not personally culpable, let us leave the matter in the Lord's hands. It is really before Him that we stand or fall.

Psalm 8

"What is Man,
That You Care For Him?"

Psalm 8

For the director of music.
According to gittith.

A Psalm of David.

1 O LORD, our Lord, how majestic is your name in all the earth!
    You have set your glory above the heavens.

2 From the lips of children and infants you have ordained praise
    because of your enemies, to silence the foe and the avenger.

3 When I consider your heavens, the work of your fingers,
    the moon and the stars, which you have set in place,
4 what is man that you are mindful of him,
    the son of man that you care for him?

5 You made him a little lower than the heavenly beings
    and crowned him with glory and honor.
6 You made him ruler over the works of your hands;
    you put everything under his feet:
7 all flocks and herds, and the beasts of the field,
8 the birds of the air, and the fish of the sea,
    all that swim the paths of the seas.

9 O LORD, our Lord, how majestic is your name in all the earth!

NIV

Psalm 8

What Is Man That You Care For Him?

This psalm speaks eloquently of the greatness of God and the dignity of man, giving to each their proper place.

I. The Greatness of God.

A. His Majesty. *"O Lord, our Lord, how majestic is your name in all the earth"*

> 1. As displayed above the heavens. *"You have set your glory above the heavens"*
> 2. As revealed to the simple. *"From the lips of children and infants you have ordained praise"*
> 3. As confounding the enemy. *"because of your enemies, to silence the foe and the avenger" (v 2).*

B. His Might. Creation is God's finger-work! *"When I consider your heavens, the work of your fingers, the moon and the stars, which you have set in place" (v 3).*

C. His Mercy.

> 1. His thought of man. *"What is man that you are mindful of him" (v 4).*
> 2. His care for man. *"the son of man that you care for him?" (v 4).*

II. The Glory of Man.

A. Man's Glory Received From God.

> 1. God the Benefactor. *"You made him ... You crowned him ... You made him ruler ... You put everything under his feet" (vv 5-6).*
> 2. Man the Beneficiary.

Position *"a little lower than the angels (or God)" (v 5)*.
Privilege *"crowned with glory and honor" (v 5)*.
Potential *"ruler over the works of your hands" (v 6)*.
Power *"everything under his feet" (v 6)*.

B. Man's Glory Ruined by the Fall. *"In putting everything under him, God left nothing that is not subject to him. Yet at present we do not see everything subject to him" (Hebrews 2:8).*

> 1. Man refused to be man on God's terms. Thus, his glory was tarnished and his authority sharply curtailed.
> 2. Man yearned for what he thought would be full freedom, and he lost what he already had.
> 3. Man himself cannot be in full control, because man himself is out of control

C. Man's Glory Restored by Christ. *"But we see Jesus, who was made a little lower than the angels, now crowned with glory and honor because he suffered death, so that by the grace of God he might taste death for everyone" (Hebrews 2:9).*

> 1. In Christ, God's Ideal Man. We see all that God wants man to be. Psalm 8 is a portrait of Him, and what man can be through Him.
> 2. Our Lord shows us that the road to power and glory is not the road of grasping ambition, but humble self—denial.

Psalm 8

What Is Man That You Care For Him?

One night long ago, a Hebrew shepherd boy, tending his flock by night, looked up into the starry heavens, and was first enthralled, then absolutely overwhelmed by the awful immensity of it all. By comparison with the vastness of the myriad twinkling stars, he shrank to a speck in the infinite, lost in space. He, a mere man. How insignificant he felt! But moved, his poet heart began to craft a song, and his fingers touched the strings of his lute, a guitar-like instrument that was his constant companion, and he sang into the starry stillness of the night.

First, he extols the greatness and majesty of Yahweh's finger work, bringing all that he beheld into existence. Then, he asks how a great God like that could give any thought to mere man. But as he sings, he remembers that man is God's masterpiece, His *poema* (poem), as Paul put it in Ephesians 2. Man really counts with God, the crown of all His creative work.

Leslie Ray Marston in his book *From Chaos to Character* has caught the wonder of God's care for man that reaches from the beginning of time to the end of time and beyond:

> "Not to save whirling worlds from collision and catastrophe; not to hinge a solar system in space; not to scoop out a Grand Canyon nor to pile high the Rockies or the Andes; but to bridge with His own Person that yawning gulf of separation between Him and man, cleft by man's mighty choice of sin, did God seek out this far-off corner of His universe, and here, by the tragic death of Himself, He spanned heaven and earth that man might be brought back to God." (*From Chaos to Character* by Leslie Ray Marston, page 13))

Plato called man a two-legged animal without feathers. James Oppenheim in his poem *Laughter* calls man "the bad child of the universe." Shakespeare has a more flattering assessment in that wonderful passage in Hamlet:

> "What a piece of work is a man! How noble in reason! How infinite in faculty! In form and moving, how express and admirable! In action how like an angel! In apprehension how like a god!"

Whether we think of man as ape or angel, dust or deity, we cannot escape the significant fact that it isn't what man is made **of**, but what he is made **for** that is vital. The Genesis record tells us that man is a creature of God, made in the image of God, a rebel against God, but destined to become a child of God, sharing the very glory of God.

Let's examine more closely David's lovely song. First, he sings of the greatness of God.

The Greatness of God

His Majesty

1. As displayed above the heavens. *"O Lord, our Lord, how majestic is your name in all the earth! You have set your glory above the heavens."* He sees the glory of God displayed **above** the heavens. If the heavens are glorious, God is more so for He made the heavens. And, remember, Psalm 19 says, *"The heavens declare the glory of God…." (v 1).* They are a silent witness to His majesty.

2. As revealed to the simple. His majesty is also recognized and declared **beneath** the heavens from the lips of "children and infants."

3. As confounding the enemy. And their praise effectively silences all those who would dare oppose God. *"… because of your enemies, to silence the foe and the avenger."* You may remember that at our Lord's entry into Jerusalem on Palm Sunday, the children cried out, *"Hosanna to the Son of David!"* and the chief priests were indignant, and said to Jesus, *"Do you hear what these children are saying?"* And Jesus replied, *"Yes, have you not read, 'From the lips of children and infants you have ordained praise'"*? And He quotes from David's psalm! And He rebukes them by saying that if the children's' lips were silenced the very stones would cry out in praise! In the Revelation, the heavenly worship team composed of the four living creatures, and the twenty-four elders, fall down before the throne and say: *"You are worthy, our Lord and God, to receive glory and honor and power, for you created all things, and by your will they were created and have their being" (4:10-11).*

Then the psalmist sings of s …

His Might

"When I consider your heavens, the work of your fingers, the moon and the stars, which you have set in place …" (v 3). He sees creation as God's finger-work. I love the graphic way James Weldon Johnson described the sequence of man's

creation in *God's Trombones*, poems based on American Negro folk sermons. God is pictured as personally fashioning man as a potter would form a piece of pottery on his wheel.

Then God walked around, and God looked around
On all that he had made.
He looked at his sun,
And he looked at his little stars;
He looked on his world with all its living things,
And God said: I'm lonely still.
Then God sat down on the side of a hill where he could think;
By a deep, wide river he sat down;
With his head in his hands,
God thought and thought, Till he thought:
I'll make me a man!
Up from the bank of the river God scooped the clay;
And by the bank of the river He kneeled him down;
And there the great God Almighty
Who lit the sun and fixed it in the sky,
Who flung the stars to the most far corner of the night,
Who rounded the earth in the middle of his hand;
This Great God, like a mammy bending over her baby,
Kneeled down in the dust toiling over a lump of clay
Till he shaped it in his own image;
Then into it he blew the breath of life,
And man became a living soul.

(*God's Trombones* by Weldon Johnson)

The moon and the stars—but also man—the finger-work of God! Then he thinks of God's love for man to thus create him in his own image and likeness.

His Mercy

"What is man that you are mindful of him, the son of man that you care for him?" Heine in his poignant poem has no answer.

O tell me what meaning has man?
Or whence he comes and whither he goes?
Who dwells beyond the golden stars?

The waves still murmur their eternal song,
The winds sigh low, the clouds pass by,
And twinkle the stars indifferent and cold,
And only a fool awaits an answer.

The psalmist read quite a different message in those stars. There is a certain glory in man, a dignity beyond calculation.

The Glory of Man.

Man's Glory Received From God

1. **God is the Benefactor.** He sees God's glory as derived from God Himself. *"You made him … You crowned him … You made him ruler … You put everything under his feet" (v 5-6).*

2. **Man is the Beneficiary**

Think of man's position! *"You made him a little lower than the angels."*
Think of man's privilege! *"You crowned him with glory and honor."*
Think of man's potential! *"You made him to rule over the work of your hands"*
Think of man's power! *"You … put everything under his feet."*

Man's Glory Ruined By the Fall

In commenting on this, the author of Hebrews quotes (2:6-8) from this psalm and then comments, *"In putting everything under him, God left nothing that is not subject to him. Yet **at present** we do not see everything subject to him" (2:8).* Why? Because of sin. Man refused to be man on God's terms. Thus, his glory was tarnished and his authority sharply curtailed. Man yearned for what he thought would be full freedom, and he lost what he already had. Man could not be in full control, because he himself was out of control.

But God had a plan already in place to restore man through His Son Jesus Christ.

Man's Glory Restored in Christ

The Hebrews commentary goes on, *"But we see Jesus, who was made a little lower than the angels, now crowned with glory and honor because he suffered death, so that by the grace of God he might taste death for everyone" (2:9).* He became what we are, in order to make us what He is! It is God's intention that through Christ's death, he might *"bring many sons to glory!"* Christ is the Ideal Man—all that God intended man should be. Psalm 8 is really a portrait of Him—the God-Man. The first man failed because of disobedience; the second Adam from above succeeded, because of perfect obedience. By Christ's death and resurrection, sin and death are soundly defeated and the way is open now for man to enjoy the glory and authority he was meant to have. Because all things are now under Christ's feet (Ephesians 2), they are also under ours since we are one with Him by faith and sit with Him in the highest place of authority. His victory has now become ours!

"O Lord, our Lord, how majestic is your name in all the earth!"

> *Father, Maker of heaven and earth, your purpose in our creation is breathtaking. How could we who were created so high stoop so low? Made "a little lower than the angels," "crowned with glory and honor," "ruler over all creation," "everything under his feet." Amazing! And yet, there is a sense in which you have now restored all of that to us. Doesn't Paul say that God has placed all things under his (Christ's) feet? And then he says that we are seated with Christ in heavenly places. Doesn't that mean that whatever is under his feet is now under ours as well? With Him in the highest place of authority! It is hard to take in—that we who were so low could rise so high!*

Something to Ponder

Is it possible for us, like Peter, to walk on water? I suppose we could do it literally, if it served God's useful purpose, but we can certainly do it spiritually! Jesus said to Peter, in effect, "Whatever is under my feet (these waves) can be under yours as well! Come to me." We have no business living "under the circumstances" if Jesus wants us to live above them with Him. But it's very important to keep our focus steady—right on Him. Looking around will bring us down.

Psalm 9

"The Lord Reigns Forever"

Psalm 9

Psalms 9 and 10 may have been originally a single acrostic poem, the stanzas of which begin with the successive letters of the Hebrew alphabet. In the Septuagint they constitute one psalm. We shall study both.

> For the director of music.
> To [the tune of] "The Death of the Son."

> A psalm of David.

1 I will praise you, O LORD, with all my heart
    I will tell of all your wonders.
2 I will be glad and rejoice in you;
    I will sing praise to your name, O Most High.

3 My enemies turn back,
    they stumble and perish before you.
4 For you have upheld my right and my cause;
    you have sat on your throne, judging righteously.
5 You have rebuked the nations and destroyed the wicked;
    you have blotted out their name for ever and ever.
6 Endless ruin has overtaken the enemy,
    you have uprooted their cities;
    even the memory of them has perished.

7 The LORD reigns forever;
    he has established his throne for judgment.
8 He will judge the world in righteousness;
    he will govern the peoples with justice.
9 The LORD is a refuge for the oppressed,
    a stronghold in times of trouble.
10 Those who know your name will trust in you, for you, LORD,
    have never forsaken those who seek you.

11 Sing praises to the LORD, enthroned in Zion;
    proclaim among the nations what he has done.

12 For he who avenges blood remembers;
    he does not ignore the cry of the afflicted.

13 O LORD, see how my enemies persecute me!
    Have mercy and lift me up from the gates of death,
14 that I may declare your praises in the gates of the Daughter of Zion
    and there rejoice in your salvation.
15 The nations have fallen into the pit they have dug;
    their feet are caught in the net they have hidden.
16 The LORD is known by his justice;
    the wicked are ensnared by the work of their hands. Higgaion. Selah
17 The wicked return to the grave,
    all the nations that forget God.
18 But the needy will not always be forgotten,
    nor the hope of the afflicted ever perish.

19 Arise, O LORD, let not man triumph;
    let the nations be judged in your presence.
20 Strike them with terror, O LORD,
    let the nations know they are but men. Selah

NIV

Psalm 9

The Lord Reigns Forever

I. An Expression of Personal Praise.

A. The nature of his praise.

It is interesting that the four phrases in verses 1 and 2 all begin with the first letter of the Hebrew alphabet which comes out in English as the fourfold "I will."

1. Adoration *"I will praise you, O LORD, with all my heart;*
2. Articulation *"I will tell of all your wonders" (v 1)*
3. Jubilation *"I will be glad and rejoice"*
4. Exultation *"I will sing praise to your name, O Most High" (v 2).*

B. The reasons for his praise. The Lord reigns, worldwide and everlasting.

The psalmists employs prophetic perfects—describing coming events as if they have already occurred, so certain is their fulfillment and so clear the victory.

1. You have defeated my enemies. *"My enemies turn back, they stumble and perish before you" (v 3).*
2. You have upheld my cause. *"For you have upheld my right and my cause;"*
3. You have righteously judged. *"For you have sat on your throne, judging righteously" (v 4).*
4. You have rebuked the wicked nations. *"You have rebuked the nations and destroyed the wicked;"*
5. You have blotted out their name. *"You have blotted out their name for ever and ever." (v 5).*
6. You have ruined the enemy. *"Endless ruin has overtaken the enemy. "You have uprooted their cities; even the memory of them has perished" (v 6).*

II. An Exhortation To Render Praise. Because the Lord reigns forever. *"The Lord **reigns** forever" (v 7).*

*"Sing praises to the Lord **enthroned in Zion;** proclaim among the nations what he has done" (v 11).*

A. He reigns supremely. *"He has established his throne for judgment" (v 7)*
B. He judges righteously. *"He will judge the world in righteousness"*
C. He governs justly. *"He will govern the peoples with justice" (v 8).*
D. He acts compassionately. *"The Lord is a refuge for the oppressed, a stronghold in times trouble. Those who know your name will trust in you, for you Lord, have never forsaken those who seek you." (v 9-10). "For he who avenges blood remembers; he does not ignore the cry of the afflicted." (v 12).*

III. An Entreaty To Enable Praise. *"that I may declare your praises" (v 14).*

A. My enemies pursue me to the gates of death. *"O LORD, see how my enemies persecute me! Have mercy and lift me up from the gates of death" (v 13).*
B. Deliver me that I may praise You in the gates of Zion. *"… that I may declare your praises in the gates of the Daughter of Zion and there rejoice in your salvation" (v 14).*

IV. A Final Plea. *"Arise, O LORD, let not man triumph …" (v 19).*

A. The defeat of the wicked.

They are self-defeating. This is the boomerang effect: they reap what they sow.

1. They fall into the pit they have dug (v 15).
2. Their feet are caught in the net they have hidden (v 15).
3. They are ensnared by the work of their hands (v 16).

They forget God. *"The wicked return to the grave, all the nations that forget God" (v 17).* This constitutes their greater sin. They have forgotten and forsaken God!

4. Don't let them triumph. *"Let not man triumph …" (v 19)*
5. Let them be judged. *"Let the nations be judged in your presence" (v 19)*

6. Strike them with terror. *"Strike them with terror, O Lord" (v 20)*
7. Let them know they are but mortal men. *"Let the nations know they are but men" (v 20)*

B. The delight of the weak.

1. The **needy** will not be forgotten by the Lord. *"But the needy will not always be forgotten" (v 18).*
2. The **afflicted** will not lose their hope in the Lord. *"Nor the hope of the afflicted ever perish" (v 18).*

Psalm 9

The Lord Reigns Forever!

Psalm 9 and 10 probably go together. There is an alphabetic arrangement that runs through both psalms, although some irregularities occur. Psalm 10 has no title as do all the psalms before and after it, and in the Septuagint (Greek) and Vulgate (Latin) translations of the Psalter, the two are combined throwing off the subsequent numbering.

The subject matter of the two psalms is somewhat different, so they will be considered separately. However, the theme that permeates both is that of the wicked nations that surround Israel, who are their avowed enemies, and who are bent on their destruction. The psalmist praises his God for judging and punishing the enemy and delivering His people. The words "wicked", "enemies," "nations," occur around 15 times in the two psalms.

In the history of Israel, there have been six successive world empires that have been determined in their efforts to destroy Israel. At the end of the age, Daniel's prophecy of the last great confederation of nations under the leadership of the Antichrist is described in the Revelation with Israel and the surviving remnant under attack again. Behind these seven great empires the sinister hand of the Dragon, Satan, can be seen. He has been fanatically obsessed with destroying the "seed of the woman" mentioned in Genesis 3:15. The seed of the woman eventually becomes Israel, the nation, through which, as a channel, the Anointed One of God—the Christ, would come (Revelation 12).

Here in Psalm 9, in spite of the oppression of the enemy, the psalmist is thankful that God is still on the throne of the universe, and very much in control of things although sometimes it may seem otherwise. *"The Lord reigns forever!"* he says. And in chapter 10, the close connection is seen as he again affirms, *"The Lord is King for ever and ever; the nations will perish from his land" (v 16).*

Psalm 9 is really all about praise. The psalmist opens by expressing his praise in two couplets, he offers reasons for praise, and then exhorts the people to render their praise, and finally, pleads for the Lord to enable his praise.

An Expression of Personal Praise.

The *nature* of his praise is expressed in four "I will" statements. First, the "I will" of *adoration. "I will praise you, O LORD, with all my heart" (v 1).* There is nothing half-hearted here, but whole-hearted, that constitutes the only proper attitude in worship. Second, there is the "I will" of *articulation*. The praise springs from the heart and finds expression in words. *"I will tell of all your wonders" (v 1)*. Next, we have the "I will" of *jubilation*. *"I will be glad and rejoice. (v 2)*. His heart is overflowing with joy! And finally, we see the "I will" of *exultation*. *"I will sing praise to your name, O Most High" (v 2)*. His joy expresses itself in song. He sets his thoughts and words to music!

Next, he offers the *reasons* for his praise. He sees his Lord reigning, world-wide and everlasting. He employs what is referred to as a prophetic perfect tense to describe events as if they had already occurred, so certain is their fulfillment and so clear the victory (Derek Kidner, *Psalms 1-72* page 69).

Notice the sequence of thought.

1. You have defeated my enemies.
2. You have upheld my right and my cause.
3. You have righteously judged.
4. You have rebuked the wicked nations.
5. You have blotted out their name.
6. You have ruined the enemy.

There is confidence in the heart of the psalmist that God will utterly defeat and destroy the enemy that oppresses the righteous.

Growing out of this comes an exhortation for the people to join him in praising the Lord, because He is enthroned—He reigns forever!

An Exhortation to Render Praise.

"Sing praises to the Lord enthroned in Zion; proclaim among the nations what he had done" (v 11). That which immediately precedes this exhortation is a recital of the reigning Lord.

He reigns supremely. *"He has established his throne for judgment" (v 7)*. His pronouncements as the Judge of the Universe are founded on His holiness and righteousness.

He judges righteously. He governs justly. *"He will judge the world in righteousness" (v. 8)*. Which means, of course, that *He will govern justly. "He will govern the peoples with justice" (v 8)*. All of which is a comfort for God's people, but not exactly what the rebellious nations want to hear. They do not want to be accountable to anyone, but themselves. They either forget God, or try to act as if He did not exist. Theirs is a practical atheism. Remember Psalm 2 where the kings and rulers gathered together against the Lord and said, *"Let us break their chains, and throw off their fetters."* The Lord is not about to let that happen!

And finally, the psalmist rehearses God's care and comfort for His afflicted people. **He acts compassionately**, the psalmist says. And there follows a couple of verses which ought to be committed to memory, *"The Lord is a refuge for the oppressed, a stronghold in times of trouble. Those who know your name will trust in you, for you Lord, have never forsaken those who seek you"* (v 9-10).

Yes, He not only reigns supremely, righteously, and justly, but He reigns compassionately. He is not aloof and uncaring.

And the psalmist breaks out into a petition to enable his personal praise.

An Entreaty to Enable Praise.

His enemies pursue him and persecute him to the very gates of death. They desire his destruction. But he cries out for mercy. *"Have mercy and lift me up from the gates of death"* (v 13). And the reason is *"... that I may declare your praises in the gates of the Daughter of Zion and there rejoice in your salvation"* (v 14). He uses this argument elsewhere—How am I going to praise you if I'm dead? Spare my life that I might declare your praises! From the gates of death to the gates of ... Zion!

A Final Plea for Action.

"Arise, O LORD, let not man triumph ..." (v 19). The psalmist often uses this expression as if to say to the Lord, "Lord, it's time for action!" He talks about how active the wicked are in their diabolical schemes, digging pits, laying down nets, trying to snare their prey like they were nothing but unsuspecting animals. But he knows their schemes are self-destructive. They have a boomerang effect: they will reap what they sow. They *"fall into the pit they have dug; their feet are caught in the net they have hidden ... they are ensnared by the work of their hands"* (v 15-16). And then he views their final end, *"They return to the grave ..."*

Their greater sin is seen in the phrase *"they have forgotten God."* There is a reckoning day just ahead, and they have forsaken their only source of help. The psalmist prays that they may be defeated, judged, stricken with terror, and made to know that they are not as invulnerable as they think. *"Let them know they are but men"* (v 20).

And in contrast to God's condemnation of the wicked, he is comforted by God's care of the weak. *"The needy will not be forgotten, nor the hope of the afflicted ever perish"* (v 18).

However circumstances sometimes seem to the contrary, God **is** mindful of His own!

Father in heaven, it is a comforting thought to know that You are "a refuge for the oppressed, a stronghold in times of trouble." Where do people turn if they cannot turn to You? Human help is often so limited and lacking, but You are unlimited in Your ability. YOU ARE ABLE! Instead of looking outward, our seeking heart looks upward, for you care about us. Thank you.

Things To Ponder

The phrase *"Those who know your name will trust in you"* reminds me of Proverbs 18:10, "The name of the Lord (Yahweh) is a strong tower; the righteous run to it and are safe." In John 8 Jesus tells us that Yahweh of the Old Testament and Y'Shua of the New are the same. *"Before Abraham was, I AM."* As the great "I AM" He gives himself away to us. All that we lack, He is to us. *"Yahweh is my Shepherd. I need lack for nothing."*

Psalm 10

"When The Wicked Seem to Triumph"

Psalm 10

1 Why, O LORD, do you stand far off?
    Why do you hide yourself in times of trouble?
2 In his arrogance the wicked man hunts down the weak,
    who are caught in the schemes he devises.
3 He boasts of the cravings of his heart;
    he blesses the greedy and reviles the LORD.
4 In his pride the wicked does not seek him;
    in all his thoughts there is no room for God.
5 His ways are always prosperous;
    he is haughty and your laws are far from him;
    he sneers at all his enemies.
6 He says to himself, "Nothing will shake me;
    I'll always be happy and never have trouble."
7 His mouth is full of curses and lies and threats;
    trouble and evil are under his tongue.
8 He lies in wait near the villages;
    from ambush he murders the innocent,
    watching in secret for his victims.
9 He lies in wait like a lion in cover;
    he lies in wait to catch the helpless;
    he catches the helpless and drags them off in his net.
10 His victims are crushed, they collapse;
    they fall under his strength.
11 He says to himself, "God has forgotten;
    he covers his face and never sees."
12 Arise, LORD! Lift up your hand, O God.
    Do not forget the helpless.
13 Why does the wicked man revile God?
    Why does he say to himself, "He won't call me to account"?
14 But you, O God, do see trouble and grief;
    you consider it to take it in hand.
The victim commits himself to you;
    you are the helper of the fatherless.

15 Break the arm of the wicked and evil man;
    call him to account for his wickedness
    that would not be found out.
16 The LORD is King forever and ever;
    the nations will perish from his land.
17 You hear, O LORD, the desire of the afflicted;
    you encourage them, and you listen to their cry,
18 defending the fatherless and the oppressed,
    in order that man, who is of the earth, may terrify no more.

NIV

Psalm 10

When The Wicked Seem To Triumph

The Psalmist's Dilemma:

"Why, O Lord, do you stand far off? Why do you hide yourself in times of trouble?" (v 1).

A sense of distance from God
A sense of desertion by God

I. The Victors. The Wicked Seem To Triumph.

A. What the wicked are like—their attitude.

1. **Arrogant** *"In his arrogance the wicked man hunts down the weak who are caught in the schemes he devises" (v 2).*
2. **Boastful** *"He boasts of the cravings of his heart; he blesses the greedy and reviles the LORD" (v 3).*
3. **Proud** *"In his pride the wicked does not seek him …" (v 4).*
4. **Rebellious** *"… in all his thoughts there's no room for God" (v 4).*
5. **Prosperous** *"His ways are always prosperous …" (v 5).*
6. **Haughty** *"He is haughty and your laws are far from him" (v 5).*
7. **Contemptuous** *"… he sneers at all his enemies" (v 5).*

B. What the wicked say—their words.

1.**No difficulty.** *"He says to himself, 'Nothing will shake me; I'll always be happy and never have trouble'" (v 6).*
2. **No scrutiny.** *"He says to himself, 'God has forgotten; he covers his face and never sees'" (v 11).*
3. **No accountability.** *"Why does he say to himself, 'He won't call me to account'"? (v 13).*

C. What the wicked do—their actions.

    1. He curses, lies, threatens, and schemes. (v. 7)
    2. He lies in wait … near villages … like a lion … to catch the helpless (v 8)
    3. He catches them, drags them off, and murders them. (v 9)

II. The Victims. The Righteous Are Weak and Oppressed.

A. Helpless *"He catches the helpless and drags them off …"* *(v 9)*
B. Defenseless *"His victims are crushed, they collapse; they fall …"* *(v 10)*.
C. Fatherless *"… the fatherless and oppressed …"* *(v 18)*.

III. The Vindicator. God Doesn't Forget the Helpless.

"Arise, LORD! Lift up your hand, O God. Do not forget the helpless" *(v 12)*.

A. God sees *"But you, O God, do see trouble and grief …"* *(v 14)*.
B. God considers *"… you consider it to take it in hand. The victim commits himself to you"* *(v 14)*.
C. God helps *"… you are the helper of the fatherless"* *(v 14)*.
D. God hears *"You hear, O LORD, the desire of the afflicted"* *"… you listen to their cry"* *(v 17)*.
E. God encourages *"… you encourage them"* *(v 17)*.
F. God defends *", defending the fatherless and the oppressed"* *(v 18)*.
G. God deals with the wicked *"Break the arm of the wicked and evil man; call him to account for his wickedness that would not be found out"* *(15)*.

"The Lord is King for ever and ever; the nations will perish from his land" *(v 16)*.

Psalm 10

When The Wicked Seem To Triumph

When we come to Psalm 10, the psalmist is faced with a dilemma: *"Why, O Lord, do you stand far off? Why do you hide yourself in times of trouble?" (v 1).* He had a sense of distance from God and of desertion by God. That's not good, is it? And the reason for his dilemma was the sense that the wicked seem to triumph over the weak and helpless.

This relationship of the strong to the weak claims our special attention because it has been the fruitful mother of the cruelest tragedies of human life. How God's heart has been grieved watching the strong squeeze the weak like grape clusters into their chalices that they might drink blood like wine! The weak, the undefended, the immature, have always been the prey of the strong. They have been ruthlessly cutup, strewn in, and plowed under to make a richer soil for the strong to grow in. The saddest chapters in history recount the story of the strong, wringing the weak dry of their toil and flinging them heedlessly aside, or displaying their power in shameless cruelties.

I suppose that is what they mean by "survival of the fittest." Empires are built for conquest, industrial systems flourish to exploit, and individual ambition can only be reached by stepping on or over fallen folk. How much of life is based on the pagan principle that the weak must bear the burdens of the strong. Someone has said, "The test of every civilization is the point below which the weakest and most unfortunate are allowed to fall."

So the psalmist is dealing here with the victors, the wicked, and the victims, the weak and oppressed. And he goes on to underline the truth that God is the vindicator of the helpless, and will deal with the wicked, and call them to account.

The Victors—The Wicked Seem to Triumph.

First, the psalmist talks about *what the wicked are like*—their attitude, **their thoughts**. And the picture he paints is not very pretty.

They are **arrogant.** *"In his arrogance the wicked man hunts down the weak, who are caught in the schemes he devises" (v 2).* They are **boastful.** *"He boasts of the cravings of his heart (his heart's desire); he blesses the greedy and reviles the LORD" (v 3).* Evil has passed the point of no return when it proclaims itself. He even speaks well of the greedy. And, of course, it should go without saying that they are characterized by **pride.** *"In his pride the wicked does not seek him …" (v 4).* They are **rebellious.** *"… in all his thoughts there is no room for God" (v 5).* We remember that pride led to rebellion when Lucifer fell from his exalted place. He is always **prosperous.** *"His ways are always prosperous …" (v 5).* That is, the things that he does seem to turn out well. He seems to always land in the winner's circle. And yet that very fact makes him **haughty and contemptuous.** *"He is haughty and your laws are far from him; he sneers at all his enemies" (v 5).*

And his basic attitude is reflected in his **words,** what he says. First, he says that *no difficulty* will beset him. *"He says to himself, 'Nothing will shake me; I'll always be happy and never have trouble'" (v 6).* And he says that there is *no scrutiny* of his actions. *"He says to himself, 'God has forgotten; he covers his face and never sees'" (v 11).* God doesn't really pay much attention to what I do, he says. And furthermore, there is *no accountability.* *"Why does he say to himself, 'He won't call me to account'"*?

He moves from thoughts, to words, and now to **deeds**, what the wicked do—their actions. They *curse, lie, threaten, and scheme. "His mouth is full of curses and lies and threats; trouble and evil are under his tongue" (v 7).* He lies in wait to pounce on his prey. *"He lies in wait near the villages; from ambush he murders the innocent, watching in secret for his victims. He lies in wait like a lion in cover …"* He catches them, drags them off, and murders them. *"… he lies in wait to catch the helpless; he catches the helpless and drags them off in his net" (v 8-9).*

After this rather extended description of the so-called victors—the wicked, he speaks of the victims—the righteous who are weak and oppressed.

The Victims—the Weak and Oppressed

They are **helpless** *"He catches the helpless and drags them off …" (v 9).*

They are **defenseless.** *"His victims are crushed, they collapse; they fall under his strength" (v 10).*

They are all alone—orphaned, **fatherless.** *"… the fatherless and oppressed" (v 18).*

The psalmist cries out, *"Arise, LORD!"* Again, it is a call for action as in Psalm 9.

The Vindicator—God Doesn't Forget The Helpless

"Lift up your hand, O God. Do not forget the helpless" (v 12). And God doesn't forget!

+ God sees. *"But you, O God, do see trouble and grief ..." (v 14).*
+ God considers. *"... you consider it to take it in hand. The victim commits himself to you ..." (v 14).*
+ God helps. *"... you are a helper of the fatherless" (v 14).*
+ God hears. *"You hear, O LORD, the desire of the afflicted"*
+ God encourages. *"... you encourage them" (v 17).*
+ God defends. *"... defending the fatherless and the oppressed" (v 18).*
+ God deals with the wicked. *"Break the arm of the wicked and evil man; call him to account for his wickedness that would not be found out" (v 15).*

"The Lord is King for ever and ever; the nations will perish from his land" (v 16).

Father, I must confess I feel like the psalmist sometimes. When things aren't working out the way I thought they should, and I face times when the darkness seems to hide your face from me, this psalm is a good one to bring to mind. Lord, I love the way it ends. You are "King for ever and ever." You are very much in charge, though it does not appear that you are sometimes. When I am weak, then you are strong! I praise you that you never leave me or forsake me. I can boldly say, "The Lord is my helper! I need not fear what men shall do to me." Thank you for being my Vindicator, my Deliverer.

Things To Ponder

When Jesus was about to return to the Father, he told his disciples that they would have to face the hostility of the world. But he told them that He would not leave them orphans. He would come to them in the person of the Holy Spirit, and not only be with them, but live in them. I love the song we sometimes sing ...

No, never alone, alone,
No, never alone.
He promised never to leave me;
Never to leave me alone.

Psalm 11

"All Other Ground is Sinking Sand"

Psalm 11

For the director of music.

Of David.

1 In the Lord I take refuge.
    How then can you say to me:
    "Flee like a bird to your mountain.
2 For look, the wicked bend their bows;
    they set their arrows against the strings
        to shoot from the shadows
        at the upright in heart.
3 When the foundations are being destroyed,
    what can the righteous do?"

4 The Lord is in his holy temple
    the Lord is on his heavenly throne.
        He observes the sons of men;
        his eyes examine them.
5 The Lord examines the righteous,
    but the wicked and those who love violence
        his soul hates.
6 On the wicked he will rain
    fiery coals and burning sulfur;
    a scorching wind will be their lot.

7 For the Lord is righteous,
    he loves justice;
    upright men will see his face.

NIV

ALL OTHER GROUND IS SINKING SAND

Psalm 11

*"When the foundations are being destroyed,
what can the righteous do?" (verse 3)*

1. The Security In The Lord. *"In the Lord I take refuge" (v. 1)*

> 1. No other refuge will do. *"How then can you say to me: 'Flee like a bird to your mountain" (v. 1).*
> 2. Without the Lord's protection, we are vulnerable to the enemy.
> *"For look, the wicked bend their bows; they set their arrows against the strings to shoot from the shadows at the upright in heart" (v. 2).*
> 3. He alone is our firm foundation. All other ground is sinking sand.
> *"When the foundations are being destroyed, what can the righteous do?" (v. 3).*

2. The Sovereignty of The Lord.

> 1. The Lord's proximity (His holy presence) *"The Lord is in his holy temple;" (v. 4) (See also Habakkuk 2:19)*
> 2. The Lord's authority (His awesome power) *"The Lord is on his heavenly throne" (v. 4).*

3. The Scrutiny of The Lord. *"He observes the sons of men; his eyes examine (tests) them" (v. 4).*

> 1. The righteous. *"The Lord examines (tries, tests) the righteous ..." (v 5).*
> 2. The wicked. *"... but the wicked and those who love violence his soul hates. On the wicked he will rain fiery coals and burning sulfur (reminiscent of Gen. 19:24); a scorching wind will be their lot" (vs. 5, 6).*

Summary Statement:

"For the Lord is righteous, he loves justice; upright men will see his face. (v. 7).

Psalm 11

All Other Ground Is Sinking Sand

"When the foundations are being destroyed, what can the righteous do?"
(Psalm 11:3).

This is still a good question for us to ask today! This psalm arises out of some crisis in David's life. I tend to agree with those who suggest it may have been during the time of the insurrection of Absalom, David's rebellious son. The foundations may refer to the stability of David's government—on shaky ground. Would the government stand or fall before the armies of Absalom?

His advisors offer him a counsel of despair suggesting that his situation was hopeless, and he ought to *"flee like a bird to your mountain."*

But David knows from past experience where his true security lies, and rejects their counsel.

The Security in the Lord

David knows that there is no other refuge. Full of unshaken faith in the Lord, he knows instinctively where to turn. The Lord may test his servants, but He will not forsake them. It is the wicked that need to fear.

David is like a bird on the branch watched by an archer who stealthily draws his bow in preparation to shoot. Instant flight is the only hope! But David knows that it does little good to run from a problem—to get away from it all. Often times we are the problem, and by getting away we take ourselves with us. Obviously, it is a good thing to get away for times of rest and relaxation, but trying to escape our problems by getting away is counter productive.

Without the protection the Lord affords—*"in the Lord I take refuge"*—David stands vulnerable before the arrows of the enemy bent on "shooting him down." When we leave the security and stability of resting in the Lord's protection, we lose our foundation. "All other ground is sinking sand." To try to build our life on any other foundation is to invite, as Jesus put it, disaster. When the storms of life blow in, it's important to find the stability that comes in building life on the Sure Foundation of the Lord.

So what is the right focus? The antistrophe that follows (Vs 4-6) tells us.

The Sovereignty of the Lord

"In His holy temple … on His heavenly throne …" (v 4).

David reminds himself, first of all, of the Lord's nearness, His **proximity.** That must be what he means when he refers to the Lord as being *"in his holy temple."* The Lord condescended to presence Himself "in the midst" of His people in the Holy of Holies between the cherubim on the Ark of the Covenant. In the wilderness march, the Lord's presence was visibly manifested in the cloud by day and the pillar of fire by night. God wanted Israel to know that He was there in their midst to provide, to pardon, and to protect them. David needed that reassurance now.

But he also reminds himself that the Lord was *"on His heavenly throne" (v 4).* This speaks, of course, of God's power and **authority.** When faced with a crisis, it is good to be reassures that God is "still on the throne." That does not mean that He is remote, but that He is in charge. It is worthwhile to remember what our Lord told His disciples as He was about to ascend to the Father, *"All power (authority) is given me … go therefore … and I will be with you always …" (Matthew 28:18-20).* So, when the situation we face seems quite hopeless, remember the promise of His power and presence with us always.

Then note, finally, how mindful our Lord is of what's happening to His own.

The Scrutiny of the Lord

"He observes the sons of men; his eyes examine (tests) them …" (v 4).

David takes comfort in the fact that the Lord takes note of what's happening to him. In fact, He was intently watching what was going on. Do we sometimes think that the Lord has more important things to do than to note the details our lives? But nothing escapes His scrutiny. That, of course, is a cause for comfort as well as concern. As for the righteous, He observes, examines, and tests them. As is seen elsewhere, His testing of the righteous is with a view to purifying them so that, as James puts it, they might develop *"perseverance"* and *"maturity"* (James 1:2-4).

But His awareness of the "violence" of wicked men is met with swift and devastating judgment like that visited on the ancient cities of Sodom and Gomorrah—*"on the wicked he will rain fiery coals and burning sulfur; a scorching wind will be their lot" (v 5, 6).*

And so David ends where he began—with the Lord. *"For the Lord is right-eous, he loves justice; upright men will see his face" (v 7).* All fear and frustration have to flee before the Righteous One. Inwardly, with the eye of faith, the Psalmist "sees" the Lord. It seems he is always gazing *"upon the beauty of the Lord" (Psalm 27:4).* His heart is ever longing for the "beatific vision" of behold-ing the face of the Lord in righteousness. *"And I—in righteousness I will see your face; when I awake, I will be satisfied with seeing your likeness" (Psalm 17:15).*

Someone has well said, "Seeking God as our refuge in trouble may some-times spring from self-regard, but seeking and seeing His face is a goal that only the pure and loving heart can desire." *"Blessed are the pure in heart, for they shall see God" (Matthew 5:8).*

Father, I confess that I am not very observant, but you are! And I thank you that you observe both the righteous and the wicked, giving to each their proper due. Oh let me see your face, and know your smile of approval on my life. Purify my heart and open my eyes that I might behold you in all your glory and beauty. I ask in your holy name. Amen

Things To Ponder

How thankful we should be that the Lord is mindful of us. He pays attention to what happens to us. He is "in His holy temple", and "on His heavenly throne." He rules in the throne room of my heart, and from His heavenly throne—King of my life, and King of the Universe!

Psalm 12

"Flattering Lips and Flawless Words"

Psalm 12

For the director of music.
According to Sheminith.

A Psalm of David.

1 Help, Lord, for the godly are no more;
     the faithful have vanished from among men.
2 Everyone lies to his neighbor;
     their flattering lips speak with deception.

3 May the Lord cut off all flattering lips
     and every boastful tongue
4 that says, "We will triumph with our tongues;
     we own our lips—who is our master?

5 "Because of the oppression of the weak
     and the groaning of the needy,
     I will now arise, says the Lord.
     "I will protect them from those who malign them."

6 And the words of the Lord are flawless,
     like silver refined in a furnace of clay
     purified seven times.

7 O Lord, you will keep us safe
     and protect us from such people forever.
8 The wicked freely strut about
     when what is vile is honored among men.

NIV

Psalm 12

Flattering Lips And Flawless Words

I. A Plea For Help. *"Help, Lord...." (v 1)*

A. He feels forsaken by his allies. *"... for the godly are no more; the faithful have vanished from among men" (v 1).*
B. He feels surrounded by his adversaries (purveyors of falsehood & flattery).

1. Empty talkers. *"Everyone lies to his neighbor"* (speaks "empty" words)
2. Smooth talkers. *"... with flattering lips ..."* ("smooth" words)
3. Double talkers. *"... and a double mind they speak."* (Lit. a heart and a heart')

II. A Prayer To Hinder. *"May the Lord cut off ..."* (put a stop to their false speech)

A. All flattering lips.
B. Every boastful tongue. *"the tongue that speaks great things"*

1. "We will have the last say!" *"We will triumph with our tongues;"*
2. "No one can tell us what to say or do!" *"We own our lips who is our master?" (v 4). "Likewise the tongue is a small part of the body, but it makes great boasts" (James 3:5)* (Note also the false prophets of 2 Peter 2)

III. A Promise To Hear. *"I will now arise ... I will protect them from those who malign them" (v 5).*

The Lord will deal with those who misuse speech, if not in this life, then in the next (Matt. 12:36).

A The Lord is mindful of the maligned. *"Because of the oppression of the weak and the groaning of the needy" (v 5).*

B. His words (promises) can be trusted. *"And the words of the Lord are flawless, like silver refined in a furnace of clay purified seven times."*
C. A concluding note of assurance. *"O Lord, you will keep us safe and protect us from such people forever."*

The wicked freely strut about when what is vile is honored among men" (v 7-8).

Psalm 12

Flattering Lips And Flawless Words

The overall thrust of Psalm 12 presents a contrast between false and flattering speech and the flawless words of God.

Words possess awesome power to hurt or heal, delight or discourage, enrage or enrich. The mouth is the billboard of the heart; words tell what we really are. Unless you, or someone dear to you, has been the victim of terrible physical violence, chances are the worst pains you have suffered in life have come from words used cruelly—from ego-destroying criticism, excessive anger, sarcasm, public and private humiliation, hurtful nicknames, betrayal of secrets, rumors, and malicious gossip.

David sees a taint spreading through society. The true glory of a country is moral, and where the moral element is lacking, all other glories are dim. To him, falsehood seemed to be everywhere, truth nowhere. David utters a simple plea for help.

A Plea for Help.

"Help, Lord …" This is a prayer like that of Peter sinking beneath the sea. The psalmist admits that his need is immediate and urgent. He senses that there aren't any that he can really depend on. *"The godly are no more; the faithful have vanished from among men" (v 1)*. He feels alone, forsaken. And instead of "the godly" and "the faithful" gathered around him, purveyors of falsehood and flattery surround him.

These are *empty talkers*. *"Everyone lies to his neighbor"* (they speak "empty" words).

They are *smooth talkers*—*"with flattering (smooth) lips …"* They use their flattery to try to deceive and manipulate.

And they are *double talkers*. *"with … a double mind they speak"* The literal meaning is "with a heart and a heart." Or maybe a modern idiom might be that they talk out of "both sides of their mouth." In other words, they aren't people of integrity; they can't be trusted. They say one thing, but really mean another.

David prays that the Lord would put a stop to their false speech.

A Prayer to Hinder. "*May the Lord cut off all flattering lips and every boastful tongue …*" *(v 3).*

Their arrogance is seen in what they say. "*We will triumph with our tongues …*" We will have the last word. We will overpower our detractors with our power of persuasion. "*We own our lips—who is our master?*" No one can tell us what to do! No one will hold us accountable!

James, in his commentary on the tongue, says, "*The tongue is a small part of the body, but it makes great boasts. Consider what a great forest is set on fire by a small spark. The tongue also is a fire, a world of evil among the parts of the body. It corrupts the whole person, sets the whole course of life on fire, and is itself set on fire by hell*" *(James 3:5-6).* Strong language, indeed! And because of the potential for harm by the wrong use of the tongue, the psalmist prays that the Lord would put a stop to their destructiveness.

It seems that the Lord responds immediately to David's plea. "*I will now arise …*"

A Promise to Hear. "*… I will protect them from those who malign them*" *(v 5).*

The Lord is not unmindful of the maligned. He knows "*the oppression of the weak and the groaning of the needy …*" *(v 5).* Just in case, we might think that no one is listening or caring about our misuse of speech, it might be good to remind ourselves again of our Lord's solemn words in Matthew 12, "*I tell you that men will have to give account on the day of judgment for every careless word they have spoken*" *(v 36).*

A Jewish folk tale, set in nineteenth-century Eastern Europe, tells of a man who went through a small community slandering the rabbi. One day, feeling suddenly remorseful, he begged the rabbi for forgiveness and offered to undergo any form of penance to make amends. The rabbi told him to take a feather pillow from his home, cut it open, scatter the feathers to the wind. The man did as he was told and returned to the rabbi. He asked, "Am I now forgiven?"

"Almost," came the response. "You just have to perform one last task: Go and gather all the feathers."

"But that's impossible," the man protested, "The wind has already scattered them."

"Precisely," the rabbi answered.

The rabbi in this story understands that words define our place in the world. Once our place—in other words, our reputation—is defined, it is very hard to change, particularly if it is negative.

President Andrew Jackson who, along with his wife was the subject of relentless malicious gossip, once noted, "The murderer only takes the life of the parent and leaves his character as a godly heritage to his children, while the slanderer takes away his goodly reputation and leaves him a living monument to his children's disgrace."

In that regard, I am reminded of what the British philosopher Bertrand Russell once noted. "Nobody ever gossips about other people's secret virtues." What most interests most people about others are their character flaws and private scandals.

Considerate, fair and civilized use of words is every bit as necessary in the larger society as in one-on-one relationships. David knew this to be true.

And he is comforted to know that the promises of the Lord can always be relied on—can be absolutely trusted. *"And the words of the Lord are flawless, like silver refined in a furnace of clay purified seven times" (v 6).* That would be an excellent verse to commit to memory, and bring to mind often!

And he reminds himself that the Lord will keep his people safe and protect them from such people. *"O Lord, you will keep us safe, and protect us from such people forever" (v 7).*

And his concluding statement underscores the truth that when wicked men and their wicked speech is ignored by those around them and not confronted, then society takes on the same bent—*"what is vile is honored among men."* And in the process, they become vile by association.

There ought to be some guide to test our use or misuse of speech. Rabbi Joseph Telushkin, rabbi of the Synagogue of the Performing Arts, offers this suggestion. He asks his audience if they can go for twenty-four hours without saying any unkind words about, or to, anybody.

Invariably, a minority of listeners raises their hands signifying "yes," some laugh, and quite a large number call out, "no!"

He responds by saying, "Those who can't answer 'yes' must recognize that you have a serious problem. If you cannot go twenty-four hours without smoking, you are addicted to nicotine. Similarly, if you cannot go for twenty-four hours without saying unkind words about others, then you have lost control over your tongue."

Want to try it?

Jesus insists that in our speech we ought to say what we mean and mean what we say. *"Anything beyond this comes from the evil one" (Matthew 5:37).*

*Lord, let the prayer of the psalmist in Psalm 19 be my prayer today,
"May the words of my mouth and the meditation of my heart be pleasing in your sight, O Lord, my Rock and my Redeemer.*

Things To Ponder

The proverb reminds us, *"He who guards his lips guards his life, but he who speaks rashly will come to ruin"* *(13:3)*. And James admonishes us, *"If anyone is never at fault in what he says, he is a perfect man, able to keep his whole body in check"* *(3:2)*. What a powerful instrument for good or ill is the tongue!

Psalm 13

"Trusting in His Unfailing Love"

Psalm 13

For the director of music.

A psalm of David.

1 How long, O LORD? Will you forget me forever?
    How long will you hide your face from me?

2 How long must I wrestle with my thoughts and
    every day have sorrow in my heart?
How long will my enemy triumph over me?

3 Look on me and answer, O LORD my God.
    Give light to my eyes, or I will sleep in death;

4 my enemy will say, "I have overcome him,"
    and my foes will rejoice when I fall.

5 But I trust in your unfailing love;
    my heart rejoices in your salvation.

6 I will sing to the LORD,
    for he has been good to me.

NIV

Psalm 13

Trusting In His Unfailing Love

A Psalm of David

This brief psalm reflects the condition of one who has faced a prolonged time of severe testing, and loses his perspective for a time. It is like one long, deep sigh at first glance. All of us, at one time or another, have felt that God has hidden His face from us and closed His ears to our cry of distress. The psalmist can help us work through these times.

I. The Problem. *"How long, O Lord?" (v. 1 & 2)*

    A. The problem of delay and detachment.

        1. Forgetfulness. *"How long … will you forget me forever?" (v 1)*.
        2. Hiddenness. *"How long will you hide your face from me? [look the other way] (v 1)*.

    B. The problem of darkness and despair.

        1. His anguished thoughts. *"How long must I wrestle with my thoughts?" (v 2)*.
        2. His aching heart. *".… and every day have sorrow in my heart" (v 2)*.

    C. The problem of defeat and disgrace. *"How long will my enemies triumph over me?" (v 2)*.

II. The Petition. *"O Lord my God …" (v 3-4)*

    A. For problem #1. Don't look the other way *"look on me"* Don't be silent any longer *"answer me"*
    B. For problem # 2 Don't keep me in the dark *"give light to my eyes"* [give me insight into this or I can't go on living!] (v 3).
    C. For problem # 3 Don't let my enemy gloat over me *"My enemy will say, 'I have overcome him,' and my foes will rejoice when I fall" (v 4)*.

III. The Praise.

A. I will trust *"in your unfailing love"*
B. I will rejoice *"in your salvation" (v 5)*
C. I will sing *"to the Lord, for he has been good to me." (v 6)*

Psalm 13

Trusting In His Unfailing Love

Obviously, we don't always feel on top of things. Living on "cloud nine" is precarious living. It doesn't last, because "cloud 10" may be a storm cloud. You've heard of "Murphy's Law" haven 't you?

> "Nothing is as easy as it looks.
> Everything takes longer than you expect.
> And if anything can go wrong, it will,
> At the worst possible moment."

Trials are common to all of us. An old French proverb says, "Sickness comes on horseback, but goes slowly away on foot." All of a sudden you may be hit with a problem, perhaps some physical ailment. But getting over it, and feeling like you are on top again may take a long time. Patience wears thin, and you're eager to be done with it.

A woman who had been ill for many days, and getting tired of her hospital stay broke down sobbing when her doctor came by to see her one morning. "How much longer am I going to have to stay here?," she demanded. His patient reply was "Just one day at a time." When you get right down to it, that's all any of us can expect. Most certainly that is all the strength God promises to give us; just one day at a time.

Psalm 13 is a song of lament, and these songs remind us that life includes both bad and good. The life of the believer is not all sweetness and light. It is when faith is recognized as being in crisis that it can be reaffirmed and strengthened. The individual songs of lament characterize almost one-third of all the psalms, and all follow a pattern that moves from a sense of desolation to delight, from grief to joy, from complaint to trust.

This short psalm reflects the condition of one who has faced a prolonged time of severe testing, and loses his perspective for a time. It signals an eclipse of the soul, and is a plea for rescue. Though it begins with a sigh, it ends with a song.

All of us at times have felt that God has hidden His face from us, and closed His ears to our cry of distress. God, of course, never really forgets or neglects His people, but it often *seems* as if He has done so. Time, to our consciousness, is relative: under stress and strain, minutes seem hours; hours, days; days, as though they would drag on their slow length for ever. David feels this keenly, but he works through it, and ends up praising the Lord for "His unfailing love."

Let's first take a look at the problems David enumerates.

The Problems.

The first problem is the problem of *delay* and *detachment.* He has the feeling that God has forgotten him, and is looking the other way, unmindful of his plight. So deep is his sense of aloneness that David asks four times in two verses, *"How long?"* And He addresses his covenant God by name, "Yahweh." Yahweh means I AM all that you need—I am present with you and available to you. He brings his predicament to the only One who can help. Always a good approach!

Forgetfulness? Hiddenness? *"How long, O Lord, will you forget me forever? How long will you hide your face from me? (v 1)?* Notice how bold David is. Sometimes in our hours of need heaven seems so unresponsive. We can't seem to penetrate the darkness to see the Savior's face.

Does God forget? Can God forget? I have been with folks lying on beds of affliction and pain who have asked those question over and over again. They feel that they have been forgotten, that God does not care, or that for some reason He has turned His back on them. What have they done to deserve this?

Forget, of course, means to lose remembrance, to be unable to recall, to omit and disregard, unintentionally perhaps, but to show neglect. Some wag has said, "Don't worry if you start to lose your memory. Why, just forget about it!" But forgetting is a terrible thing.

We are so prone to forget, but God—never! Jesus said one day to his disciples, whom He had been preparing for hardship and persecution up ahead, *"Are not five sparrow sold for two farthings, and **not one of them is forgotten before God,** and even the very hairs of your head are numbered. Fear not, therefore, you are of more value than many sparrows."* No, they wouldn't be alone. God would not forget His own!

I love God's simile of motherhood in Isaiah 49:15, *"Can a mother forget the baby at her breast and have no compassion on the child she has borne? Though she may forget, **I will not forget you!** See, I have engraved you on the palms of my hands ..."* There is nothing about us easier to see than the palm of our own hands. That's the figure. We are always before Him!

Next, there is the problem of *darkness* and *despair.* *"How long must I wrestle with my thoughts and everyday have sorrow in my heart"* (v 2)? His thoughts are anguished; his heart is aching. David had seen the Lord's hand powerfully work for him in the past, but now he questions. We understand David, because it is so easy for us to lose our focus when things go awry and our way grows dark. Thoughts can be destructive as well as constructive. We can think our way into bitterness. Perhaps if we would change ever so slightly the word "disappointment" to "His appointment" it might help us understand that even the trial we are undergoing may be His blessed appointment for us, and we can look for the blessing in it.

Finally, David faces the problem of **defeat** and **disgrace.** "*How long will my enemy triumph over me*" *(v 2)?* Does the opposition seem overwhelming sometimes? Perhaps we think that this trial is too much for us to bear. The enemy of our soul seems to have won again. Remember what Paul wrote in I Corinthians 10, "*God is faithful; He will not let you be tempted beyond what you can bear. But when you are tempted, he will also provide a way out so that you can stand up under it*" *(v 13).* Sometimes, we're our own worst enemy. Remember the cartoon character Pogo who announces, "We have met the enemy, and he is us!" Our own flesh so often conquers us, and when the flesh is concerned, everything becomes an enemy. Is that besetting sin getting you down again?

And at this point the psalmist cries out to the Lord. His panic turns to petition.

The Petition.

His prayer mirrors his problems. For the problem of **delay and detachment**, he prays, "Don't look the other way—**look on me.**" Note it is very personal. And "Don't be silent any longer—**answer me.**"

To the problem of *darkness and despair*, he prays, in effect, "Don't keep me in the dark any longer." "*Give light to my eyes.*" In other words, give me some insight into this or I simply can't go on—"*I will sleep in death.*"

And finally, he petitions, in regard to the third problem, the problem of *defeat and disgrace*, "Don't let my enemy gloat over me." "*My enemy will say, 'I have overcome him,' and my foes will rejoice when I fall*" *(v 4).* Lord, don't let that happen!

And finally, the petition blends into praise.

The Praise.

What a delightful change of mood—from sadness to gladness. He cries, "*I will trust.*" Trust in what? "*In your unfailing love.*" He has his focus back, doesn't he? "*I will rejoice in your salvation!*" "*I will sing to Yahweh for He has been good to me (dealt bountifully with me)*" *(v 6).* The sense of gloom and doom is past.

The problems may not have dissipated, but he senses the Lord's presence and the Lord's pleasure and the Lord's power, and He lifts his voice in song.

> *Lord, I remember someone telling me once that it isn't so much what happens to us, but what we do with what happens to us after it happens. I know that is true, but it's easy to forget when your going through it. The answer is in you and your unfailing love. Help me work my way out of sadness into gladness by looking to you. Amen.*

Things To Ponder

Knowing that God's love is constant, that it doesn't fluctuate back and forth, is a comfort. **It is unfailing.** Other things may fail, but not His love!

Psalm 14

"No One Does Good—
Not Even One"

Psalm 14

For the director of music.

Of David.

1 The fool says in his heart, "There is no God."
    They are corrupt, their deeds are vile; there is no one who does good.

2 The LORD looks down from heaven on the sons of men
    to see if there are any who understand, any who seek God.

3 All have turned aside; they have together become corrupt;
    there is no one who does good, not even one.

4 Will evildoers never learn—
    those who devour my people as men eat bread
    and who do not call on the LORD?

5 There they are, overwhelmed with dread,
    for God is present in the company of the righteous.

6 You evildoers frustrate the plans of the poor,
    but the LORD is their refuge.

7 Oh that salvation for Israel would come out of Zion!
    When the LORD restores the fortunes
    of his people, let Jacob rejoice and Israel be glad!

NIV

Psalm 14

No One does Good—Not Even One!

I. The Fool Exposed. By the Psalmist *"The fool says in his heart, "There is no God."*

    A. The fool's confession *"No God"*
    B. The fool's nature *"They are corrupt"*
    C. The fool's conduct *"their deeds are vile"*
    D. The fool's companions *"there is no one who does good" (v 1)*

II. The Fool Observed. By God

    A. What is He looking for?

        1. To see if anyone understands
        2. To see if anyone seeks God (v 2)

    B. What does He find?

        1. All have turned aside
        2. They have together become corrupt
        3. No one does good, not even one. (v 3)

III. The Fool Deluded. Self-deluded

    A. He never learns. *"Will evildoers never learn?" (v 4)*
    B. He preys on God's people. *"… those who devour my people as men eat bread" (v 4)*
    C. He does not pray to God. *"… and who do not call on the Lord?" (v 4).*
    D. He lives in nameless dread, because God is with His people. *"There they are, overwhelmed with dread," (v 5)*
    E. He mistreats the poor, but God is their refuge. *"You evildoers frustrate the plans of the poor, but the Lord is their refuge" (v 6)*

IV. A Prayer.

A. That Israel might be saved. *"Oh, that salvation for Israel would come out of Zion!" (v 7)*.

B. That the fortunes of Israel might be restored. *"When the Lord restores the fortunes of his people …"*

C. That Israel would rejoice and be glad when the Lord does this. *"… let Jacob rejoice and Israel be glad!" (v 7)*

Psalm 14

No One Does Good—Not Even One

It should be noted at the outset that this psalm is repeated as Psalm 53. The New Testament commentary on these psalms is Romans 3:10-12 where Paul declares all men, Jew and Gentile, under sin's dominion and power. Men of the world don't like to hear that verdict. And so they deny that God exists or at least they live like He doesn't.

God made us; He made the world, and all that is in it; and to deny that He exists, and to ignore His will is immorality of the profoundest kind. All sin is directed against God, and if man had his wish, he would eliminate God so that he could sin with impunity and without responsibility. *"Their foolish heart was darkened,"* Paul says in Romans 1:21. Then he quotes from this ancient psalm to show the apostasy of both Jews and Gentiles from their God, and to prove them to be all under sin. God is the "salt" of human nature, and when He is denied, man rapidly corrupts. Atheism cannot produce a noble man. It creates a fool. We sin against God, then we try to forget Him; we forget Him, and then we deny Him. Sin results in a man sinking into a sort of practical atheism.

Here in Psalm 14, the psalmist first exposes the practical atheist for what he really is.

The Fool Exposed

The principle by which wicked men live is here given. *"There is no God."* And their practice matches their principle, *"They are corrupt, their deeds are vile; there is no one who does good" (v. 1).* The psalmist calls such "fools."

Now it should be noted that it is not a light thing to call a man a fool. To do so, Jesus says, makes a person liable to hell's fire (Matthew 5:22). It is a word that strikes deeply at a man's character. The Greek word is the word from which we get the derogatory designation, "He's a moron!" It designates a person a rebel or a scoundrel. And since human personality, made in God's likeness, is precious, such names are inappropriate.

The psalmist, however, does not hesitate to use the designation for wicked men. The Hebrew word for 'fool' is *nabal.* David had a run-in with a Nabal, you remember, who refused to help him and his men when in desperate trouble.

A fool is not a person who lacks information, or intelligence, or judgment. Such a person needs our understanding and patient instruction. But a fool, as the Bible sees him, is one who is stubborn, rebellious, and disobedient. He knows what to do, but deliberately refuses to do it. He rationalizes wrong conduct. His attitudes are willfully wicked, his deeds vile.

Nor does the Biblical fool debate the existence of God. He lives and acts as though God does not exist. He is a practical atheist not a theoretical atheist. His opposite is described in Hebrews 11:6 as one who draws near to God, believes that He exists and that He rewards those who diligently seek Him.

Since what we believe shapes what we do, a fool's belief or lack of belief issues in corrupt conduct. When a fool denies God, he thinks he is free to make up his own rules, set up his own values and standards. But with no moral absolutes, he becomes vulnerable to sinful urges that issue in sinful habits. In the eyes of the psalmist, he is a vile person.

The observation of an all-seeing God confirms what the Psalmist has already observed.

The Fool Observed

"The Lord looks down from heaven on the sons of men to see if there are any who understand, any who seek God" (v 2).

In Noah's time, God carefully searched the world over, but found only one man who was righteous and a man of faith. That was almost 2,000 years after man was created. But He did find one, and spared eight souls in all. That God does not punish blindly is seen also in Sodom's destruction. Before it was overthrown, visitors were sent to see if there were any righteous souls there before wrath was poured out. God found only Lot, and spared him and his family (even Lot's wife failed to make it).

Here God looks down. There must be a few who are righteous, since they are mentioned in context, but generally His verdict was and is *"there aren't any who understand or any who seek God. They have all turned aside, they have together become corrupt; there is no one who does good, not even one" (v 2, 3).* That is a statement of the total corruption of the children of Adam, embracing all without exception. This is how Paul interprets the psalmist, saying that men everywhere are corrupt (Romans 3:10-12). The source is polluted; the waters are poisoned at the spring. The life is depraved. When our first parents renounced God in the garden, they were saying, in effect, to God, "We don't need you for our lives. We can direct our own destinies. Look where it led them in the days of the flood! If in Psalm 8 we have a picture of the *ideal* man, the *original* man, but here we have a picture of the *actual* man. God created man so high, but he sank so low!

The following strophe shows what the evil heart proposes. It persecutes those who are righteous, and those who are the objects of God's special care.

The Fool Deluded

"Will evildoers never learn—those who devour my people as men eat bread and who do not call on the Lord? There they are, overwhelmed with dread, for God is present in the company of the righteous. You evildoers frustrate the plans of the poor, but the Lord is their refuge" (v. 4-6).

These "workers of iniquity", while preying on the helpless, omit praying to God. Those bound in evil instinctively hate those who are righteous, and attack those weaker than themselves. Like eagles prey on smaller birds, and like larger fish devour smaller fish, these evildoers eat the people of God like they would eat bread.

But they don't have it all their own way. A panic seizes them at times: an indefinable, nameless terror. All cruel men are at heart cowards. It is an irksome thing for them to perceive that God is with the righteous, and against them. The New Testament affirms that those who pierce the people of God wound the Savior as well. Their judgment is sure. Verse 6 says that they mock the poor. They say, "What can your God do for you now? Where is He when you need Him most?" Patience is required, but God will vindicate His own.

And this reminds the psalmist to offer a prayer for deliverance.

The Prayer

"Oh, that salvation for Israel would come out of Zion! When the Lord restores the fortunes of his people, let Jacob rejoice and Israel be glad!" (v 7).

Notice, he says 'when' not 'if.' God's timing is not always ours. Messiah's coming has been the hope of the godly in all ages. The prophetic word is that the Lord will come to Mount Zion, and a remnant of Israel will believe, call on the name of the Lord, and be saved. And the Church also longs and looks for His coming for rapture, resurrection, and reward.

And great joy is associated with that climactic event at the end of the age. Then the wicked will be decisively judged, and the righteous will receive their long awaited reward. Even so come, Lord Jesus!

Father, may Zechariah's prophecy be fulfilled soon when the Lord's feet touch the Mount of Olives, and the remnant of Israel finally believe and receive their Messiah. Then the New Covenant blessings will come upon your people, and you will remember their sin no more. What a glorious day that will be!

Things To Ponder

I saw a bumper sticker the other day with the traditional sign of a Christian, the fish, changed to a fish with legs and the name "Darwin" where "Jesus" should have been. This is an obvious a slam at God and creationism. I couldn't help but feel a bit sad at this attempt to discredit God. Such will have their day to answer for their unbelief.

Psalm 15

"Living in God's Presence"

Psalm 15

A psalm of David.

1 LORD, who may dwell in your sanctuary?
    Who may live on your holy hill?

2 He whose walk is blameless
    and who does what is righteous,
    who speaks the truth from his heart
3 and has no slander on his tongue,
    who does his neighbor no wrong
    and casts no slur on his fellowman,
4 who despises a vile man
    but honors those who fear the LORD,
    who keeps his oath even when it hurts,
5 who lends his money without usury
    and does not accept a bribe against the innocent.

He who does these things will never be shaken.

NIV

Psalm 15

Living In God's Presence

I. Such A Person Lives Blamelessly. (Our Walk—what we are.) *"He whose walk is blameless ..." (v 2).* (free from the pointing finger!)

> **A. He is a person of his word.** *"Who keeps his oath even when it hurts" (v 4).*
> **B. He is fair and compassionate in his treatment of others.** "*... who lends his money without usury (interest)" (v 5).*
> **C. He doesn't hurt others to benefit himself.** "*... does not accept a bribe against the innocent" (v 5).*

II. Such A Person Acts Righteously. (Our Work—what we do.) *"He ... who does what is righteous ..." (v 2).*

> The righteous man is the man who acts in an honorable way!

> **A. He detests the man who cuts corners.** "*... who despises a vile man" (v 4).*
> **B. He delights in those who fear the Lord.** "*... but honors those who fear the Lord" (v 4).*

> The fear of the Lord is the beginning of wisdom. Whatever is not right is wrong, and wrong has inevitable consequence because it is out of sync with the divine nature of things.

III. Such A Person Speaks Truthfully. (Our Words—what we say. "*... who speaks the truth from his heart" (v 2).*

> This man is a man of integrity. What he says is one with what he is.

> **A. He does not run others down verbally either to their face or behind their back.** "*... who has no slander on his tongue" (v 3).*
> **B. He doesn't take advantage of his neighbor.** *"He does his neighbor no wrong" (v 3)*
> **C. He speaks well of him. His speech is constructive.** *"He casts no slur on his fellowman" (v 4)*

Psalm 15

Living In God's Presence

Our psalm for study begins with King David posing a question to the Lord about temple worshipers, *"O Lord, who may dwell in your tent? Who may live on your holy hill?* He is asking, "What kind of person will God welcome into His presence to worship Him?"

Today we might answer David's question by replying, "A Christian. A believer. A man or woman of God." Certainly, any person who has accepted Christ by faith is welcome in God's presence. The psalmist, however, is not dealing with the issue of salvation, but how a believer should live daily in order to be able to worship God in spirit and in truth. What is such a person like? How does such a person live?

It is important to ask this for two reasons: First, it deals with practical living. Interestingly, the qualities David discovers in this psalm closely parallel the qualities that Paul describes for elders and deacons in I Timothy and Titus. They offer a practical description of the believer and how he or she should relate to people around them. There is a close connection between the horizontal and the vertical relationship, that is, we cannot worship God, and wrangle with men at the same time. Notice how John puts it in his first epistle chapter 5 and verse 1, *"Everyone who loves the Father loves his child as well."*

Second, it is an important question because of the benefits of being welcome in God's presence. In the Old Testament culture, to be welcome in someone's house meant enjoying the benefits of Oriental hospitality—namely protection and sustenance. So here in Psalm 15, David is asking, "Who is welcome in God's presence? Who will God approve and delight in? The psalmist tells us.

The one who is welcome in God's presence....

1. Lives blamelessly—this has to do with our walk—what we are.
2. Acts righteously—this has to do with our work—what we do.
3. Speaks truthfully—this has to do with our words—what we say.

In verses 3 to 5, we have an explanation of these three characteristics:

Such A Person Lives Blamelessly

The New International Version translates it, *"He whose walk is blameless,"* while the New American Standard Version reads, *"He who walks with integrity."* They both suggest that such a person is the kind at whom no one can point an accusing finger and say, "Just look what he did or didn't do!" "Did you hear what she said?" "Did you see how he treated her?" Such a person has a good reputation before his fellow men and seeks to please God in what he says or does. He "walks in integrity" in the sense that his life has one motive that drives it—that of pleasing the Lord. He isn't divided or fragmented but wholly committed to the purpose and plan of God.

The last part of verse 4 and verse 5 give some concrete examples of this kind of walk. "*Who keeps his oath even when it hurts.*" He is a person of his word. He keeps his promises even if it isn't convenient or if it is costly to him personally to do so. If the circumstances change so that he is put at a disadvantage, he still keeps his word. He is trustworthy. You remember that our Lord placed a high priority on being a person of your word in Matthew 5, "*Simply let your 'Yes' be "Yes,' and your 'No,' No'; anything beyond this comes from the evil one" (v 37).* Say what you mean and mean what you say!

Then the psalmist gives a second example, "*Who lends his money without usury (interest)*" *(v 5).* He doesn't add to the burden of a destitute friend, by adding interest payments on to a loan. He is fair and compassionate in his treatment of others.

Still a third example is offered in the words "*Who does not accept a bribe against the innocent*"*(v 5).* Such a person is honest in his business deals. He doesn't take kickbacks. He is not susceptible to outside influence or corruption. He doesn't hurt others in order to benefit himself. You get the feeling that here is one who treats others, as he himself wants to be treated. This has a lot to say to the Christian businessman in the workplace.

So living blamelessly has to do with our walk, our manner of life before a watching world.

Such A Person Acts Righteously

"*Who does what is righteous*" or "*who works righteousness.*" *(v 2).* This means that such a person acts in a right and honorable manner. He doesn't cheat on his income tax. His life is characterized by "good deeds." He sees human need, and evaluates his own abilities and resources, and if it is possible for him to help in some way, he gladly does so. He does not say, "I am only one—what can I do?" But rather, "I am one—I can make a difference where I am and with what I have." He makes himself a part of the solution rather than the problem. His life is governed by personal honesty.

Verse 4 characterizes such a person as one *"who despises a vile man."* He has no use for the man who cuts corners and tries to get rich at other people's expense. On the other hand, *"he honors those who fear the Lord."* The apostle Paul, you may remember, said a similar thing in his great love chapter (I Corinthians 13), *"Love does not delight in evil but rejoices in the truth. It always protects, always trusts, always hopes, and always perseveres" (v 6, 7).*

So, in addition to living blamelessly and acting righteously …

Such A Person Speaks Truthfully

"Who speaks the truth from his heart" (v 2). Notice that what is said is spoken from the heart. It is not just outward speech, but what is said springs from a fountain of integrity and truth. Proverbs 23:7 tells us that as a man thinks in his heart, so is he. We often say, "I didn't mean to do that or say that." And yet, what is within will eventually come out. Jesus says, "A tree is known by its fruit.

Again, David offers some concrete examples of this kind of truthfulness in verse 3. *"Who has no slander on his tongue."* Such a person doesn't run others down verbally, whether in their presence or behind their back. He isn't a gossip. He either says something constructive about another, or he keeps quiet, realizing that there is always one fact more that he doesn't know about that person. Someone has said, "We would love each other better if we only understood."

Furthermore, *"He does his neighbor no wrong."* He doesn't take advantage of his neighbor. He is careful to cultivate good will. He returns borrowed tools, and is grateful for courtesies rendered him. He doesn't complain or quibble about matters of little consequence.

And finally, *"He casts no slur on his fellow man."* Actually, the progression here is quite interesting. "Neighbor," "friend," and "intimate (or one near you)." He treats everyone fairly and honestly. He speaks well of his neighbor, friend or intimate acquaintance. Both the Proverbs and the apostle Paul remind us that our words can either help or hurt others. The man who honors God, James tells us, uses his tongue constructively rather than letting it get wildly out of control.

In the eyes of the world, then, men and women are often measured by outward appearance and activities. In God's eyes, men and women are measured by their character—what they are, what they do, and what they say.

Who is welcome in God's presence? A Christian, a man or woman of God, to be sure, but beyond that, those who walk blamelessly, act righteously, and speak truthfully.

And the psalmist summarizes what he has said by saying, *"He who does these things will never be shaken—will never lose his secure foundation."* Such a person is a stable person, a person of strength, to whom others come when their foundations are shaking. The wind and the waves beat upon such a house and it holds firm because its foundations are sure!

> *Father, I desire to be a genuine person, so that those around me will see that in my work, my walk, and my words, I seek to be diligent, trustworthy and honest. Let me not stoop to devious methods to gain my personal ends, but seek always and only to live life constructively so that others will be helped and encouraged by my life. Amen.*

Things To Ponder

What I do outwardly always reflects what I am inwardly. A tree is known by its fruit. If the source is pure, that which flows from us will be refreshing, safe for all to drink.

Psalm 16

"Seeking Life's Highest Good"

Psalm 16

A miktam of David.
(A personal or private prayer)

1 Keep me safe, O God, for in you I take refuge.

2 I said to the LORD, "You are my Lord;
    apart from you I have no good thing."

3 As for the saints who are in the land,
    they are the glorious ones in whom is all my delight.

4 The sorrows of those will increase who run after other gods.
    I will not pour out their libations of blood
    or take up their names on my lips.

5 LORD, you have assigned me my portion and my cup;
    you have made my lot secure.

6 The boundary lines have fallen for me in pleasant places;
    surely I have a delightful inheritance.

7 I will praise the LORD, who counsels me;
    even at night my heart instructs me.

8 I have set the LORD always before me.
    Because he is at my right hand, I will not be shaken.

9 Therefore my heart is glad and my tongue rejoices;
    my body also will rest secure,

10 because you will not abandon me to the grave,
    nor will you let your Holy One see decay.

11 You have made known to me the path of life;
    you will fill me with joy in your presence,
    with eternal pleasures at your right hand.

NIV

Seeking Life's Highest Good

Psalm 16

All that is good is found in God. If a man has God as his portion, he needs nothing else. No one ever makes God supreme and suffers loss.

I. The Lord—The Ultimate Measure. *"Keep me safe, O God, for in you I take refuge" (v 1)*

> **A. He delights in the Person of God.** *"I said to the Lord, "You are my Lord; apart from you I have no good thing" (v 2).* Literal translation: Good for me, none besides Thee.
> **B. He delights in the People of God.** *"As for the saints who are in the land, they are the glorious (noble) ones in whom is all my delight" (v 3).*
> **C. There is no alternative to God.** *"The sorrows of those will increase who run after **other gods.** I will not pour out their libations of blood or take up their names on my lips" (v 4).*

II. The Lord—The Ultimate Treasure.

> **A. The Lord is his Portion for life.** *"Lord, you have assigned me **my portion** and my cup; you have made **my lot** secure. The boundary lines have fallen for me in pleasant places; surely I have a delightful inheritance" (v 5-6).*
> **B. The Lord is his Counselor for life.** *"I will praise the Lord, **who counsels me;** even at night my heart instruct me" (v 7)*
> **C. The Lord is his Companion for life.** *"I have set the Lord always before me. Because he is at **my right hand,** I will not be shaken" (v 8).*

III. The Lord—The Ultimate Pleasure.

> **A. This lasting pleasure extends beyond the grave.** *"Therefore **my heart** is glad and **my tongue** (my glory) rejoices; my **body** also will rest secure, because you will not abandon me (my soul) to the grave (Hades), nor will you let your Holy One see decay" (v 9-10).*

+ my heart—already rejoices
+ my glory—already exults
+ my flesh—will rest securely (resurrection intended)

B. The Source of lasting pleasure. *"You have made known to me the path of life"*
C. The Secret of lasting pleasure. *"… you will fill me with joy in your presence (with thy face)"*
D. The Sphere of lasting pleasure. *"… with eternal pleasures (delight) at your right hand" (v 11).*

Psalm 16

Seeking Life's Highest Good

"I said to the Lord, "You are my Lord; Apart from you I have no good thing." (v 2).

The Psalmist asserts in this familiar psalm that no one ever makes God supreme in life and suffers loss. The great apostle says the same thing. He had suffered the loss of all things he formerly found important, and counted them as so much garbage that he might win Christ. The apostle as well as the psalmist had taken a good look at other choices in life and found them wanting. They knew that life demands we make a choice, and they see their surrender to God as a happy choice.

A rich young ruler came to Jesus one day, and addressed him as *"Good Master …"* And Jesus replied, *"Why do you call me good? None is good except God alone."*

Jesus was saying, in effect, "You call me good, and if you confess me to be good, you must admit me to be God. And if I am your God, then I shall expect the supreme place in your life. And if I am supreme in your life, there can be nothing in competition. Go and sell all you have, and give to the poor, and great shall be your reward. And come, follow me." The man went away sadly, for he had great possessions. Jesus wanted his disciples to learn from this that no man ever makes Him supreme and suffers loss. Someone has said, "When a man holds on, God takes away; when a man lets go, God gives, and that quite liberally."

The Lord—The Ultimate Measure

The Lord's Person.

The psalmist begins this psalm by affirming, *"You are my Lord."* He will go on later to enlarge on that, but having affirmed it, he then proceeds to say that having the Lord, he needs nothing else. A literal translation of what he says is, *"Good for me there is none besides Thee."* What a tremendous thought! The one who has God as his portion needs nothing else simply because all that is really good is encompassed in God. Could that have been what the apostle Paul meant when in Colossians 2 he said, *"In Christ there is all of God in a human body; **so you have everything when you have Christ …"*** Not Christ plus something else!

When our first parents sinned in the garden, they lost more than their place in the garden. They lost their union with God. Man has tried to fill the empty vacuum in the center of his life with alternative deities—egotism, materialism, and sensualism, but nothing else really satisfies. The psalmist puts it bluntly, *"The sorrows of those will increase who run after other gods ..." (v 4).* So it has ever been! The psalmist has taken a good look at all the other choices in life and found them wanting. When it comes to real satisfaction, idols have nothing whatever to offer. He has made his happy choice to surrender himself to God's loving care.

> Good for me
> None besides Thee!

The Lord's People

Note, not only does he delight in the Lord's Person, but also he delights in the Lord's People "the fellowship of kindred hearts." These "noble" ones fill him with great joy. And he immediately speaks of the grief of those who run after other gods. There is simply no substitute for the Lord. He is the absolute indispensable One. The psalmist could not imagine anything or anyone replacing the Lord in his affections.

Jesus made this principle very clear in His teachings. No man can serve two Masters at the same time. God must have our exclusive love and devotion, and that is because He is God.

In the second place, the psalmist asserts that ...

The Lord—The Ultimate Treasure

"The boundary lines have fallen for me in pleasant places; surely I have a delightful inheritance." (v 6) The psalmist means the Lord is his **Portion** for life. This follows closely on his repudiation of any other god. David reproaches Saul in I Samuel 26:19, *"... they have driven me out ... that I should have no share in the heritage of the Lord, saying, 'Go, serve other gods.'"* God gave the priests no territory they could call their own, but assured them, *"I am your portion and your inheritance" (Num. 18:20).* Here David asserts that the Lord is his heritage. Of course, this is true for every child of God. All that God has for us is bound up in Jesus Christ, His Son. Paul delights to speak of that inheritance—the exceeding riches of His grace. My inheritance is *"fair to me"* says the psalmist.

This inheritance also includes that the Lord is his **Counselor** for life. *"I will praise the Lord, who counsels me; even at night my heart instructs me" (v 7)*. He has the sense of God's consistent guidance along the way. Even his sleep is sometimes interrupted for instruction from the Lord.

Then he adds the thought that the Lord is his **Companion** for life. *"I have set the Lord always before me. Because he is at my right hand, I will not be shaken (or not be moved)" (v. 8)*. He senses the continual presence of the Lord. The "right hand" is the place of honor. The Lord is there with him to stand by him in all the changing vicissitudes of life. As a result he is perfectly secure: he will *"not be moved or shaken."* How reminiscent of our Lord's words to his disciples, *"I will never leave you or forsake you ... I will be with you always."* What a wonderful assurance!

Finally, the psalmist refers to the Lord as The Ultimate Pleasure in this life and the next.

The Lord—The Ultimate Pleasure.

That is the blessed life of the believer who is yielded to the Lord.

What about death? It always seems to loom just over the horizon, whether near or far. But even here there is unspeakable felicity as his portion. The Old Testament has no clear-cut doctrine of immortality, but the truth appears in flashes and broken lights in many places. His lasting pleasure, David says, **extends even beyond the grave.** *"Therefore my heart is glad and my tongue rejoices; my body will rest secure, because you will not abandon me (my soul) to the grave (Hades), nor will you let your Holy One see decay" (v 9-10)*.

> + my heart—already rejoices
> + my glory—already exults
> + my flesh—will rest securely (resurrection intended)

David is rejoicing that God will not simply forsake him to the power of death. God will not let him see destruction. He believes that he will have nothing to fear from death. So much for David's own personal confidence. But we are aware from the New Testament that Peter considered this a reference to Christ. In Acts 2:25-28 he quotes this passage, and then comments that David is dead and buried. David's body has not yet been raised. Hence, Peter concludes David is speaking prophetically concerning the resurrection of Christ. Later Paul, speaking in Antioch of Pisidia, quotes these same words. He speaks with great definiteness that David died and saw corruption, but Christ whom

God raised saw no corruption. Christ's body was preserved so that corruption did not even set in whereas David's body actually must have seen corruption as all bodies do. And we too may rejoice that though our bodies may die and see corruption, they will not be permanently destroyed. The glad day is coming when *"this corruptible must put on incorruption, and this mortal must put on immortality"* (I Corinthians 15:53). The Lord Jesus at His coming will change the body of our humiliation that it may be fashioned like unto the body of His glory (Phil. 3:20-21).

The psalmist is stressing that if we are to experience pleasures forevermore, we must recognized that the Lord is our only abiding asset in this life or the next.

David sees God as **the Source of lasting pleasure.** *"You have made known to me the path of life."* He shows us the way, and He Himself is the Way. Because He lives, we too shall live!

And God is also **the Secret of lasting pleasure.** *"… you will fill me with joy in your presence (with your face)."* Jesus referred to His joy as He sought to comfort His disciples on the eve of His death. *"These things have I spoken unto you, that my joy might remain in you, and that your joy might be full"* (John 15:10-11).

> In the secret of His presence
> How my soul delights to hide!
> Oh, how precious are the lessons
> Which I learn at Jesus' side!

And finally, he sees God as **the Sphere of lasting pleasure.** *"… with eternal pleasures (delights) at your right hand" (v. 11).*

In Psalm 110:1 the right hand of God is the place of **authority and power.** *"The Lord said unto my Lord, Sit at my right hand, until I make your enemies your footstool."*

A simple cross-reference tells me further that the right hand of God is the place of **security.** *"You give me your shield of victory (salvation); and your right hand sustains me, and your gentleness (stooping down) has made me great" (Psalm 18:35).*

And still again, Psalm 98:1 describes the right hand of God as the place of **victory.** *"… his right hand and his holy arm has worked salvation (victory) for him."*

Someone has said, "Go with God; you'll thoroughly enjoy the trip!" God calls us to rich friendship with himself. Our deepest needs are met; our sorest hurts are healed. True happiness demands that we choose. **"You are my Lord; I have no good apart from you.**

Father, teach me that everything exists for you; that it's not about me, but you. You are the Ultimate Measure for life. Teach me also that everything belongs to you; you are the Sole Possessor of all thing, the Ultimate Treasure. All that I possess is a gift from your gracious hand. I hold it in trust.

Things To Ponder

Surely, the Lord wants us to be people of integrity with nothing dividing or fragmenting our lives—no competing or alternate centers allowed. The Lord is the great totalitarian of the soul. He wants us to love him with all our heart, our soul, and our mind.

Psalm 17

"The Pure in Heart See God"

Psalm 17

A prayer of David.

1 Hear, O LORD, my righteous plea; listen to my cry.
    Give ear to my prayer—it does not rise from deceitful lips.
2 May my vindication come from you;
    may your eyes see what is right.

3 Though you probe my heart and examine me at night,
    though you test me, you will find nothing;
    I have resolved that my mouth will not sin.
4 As for the deeds of me—by the word of your lips
    I have kept myself from the ways of the violent.
5 My steps have held to your paths;
    my feet have not slipped.

6 I call on you, O God, for you will answer me;
    give ear to me and hear my prayer.
7 Show the wonder of your great love,
    you who save by your right hand
    those who take refuge in you from their foes.
8 Keep me as the apple of your eye;
    hide me in the shadow of your wings

9 from the wicked who assail me,
    from my mortal enemies who surround me.
10 They close up their callous hearts,
    and their mouths speak with arrogance.
11 They have tracked me down,
    they now surround me, with eyes alert,
    to throw me to the ground.
12 They are like a lion hungry for prey,
    like a great lion crouching in cover.

13 Rise up, O LORD, confront them, bring them down;
    rescue me from the wicked by your sword.

14 O LORD, by your hand save me from such men,
from men of this world whose reward is in this life.
You still the hunger of those you cherish;
their sons have plenty, and they store up wealth for their children.
15 And I (as for me)—in righteousness I will see your face;
when I awake, I will be satisfied with seeing your likeness.

NIV

The Pure In Heart See God

Psalm 17

"Blessed are the pure in heart, for they will see God" (Matthew 5:8).

I. The Cry Of The Pure In Heart. *"Hear, O LORD …"*

  A. Listen to me.

      1. Hear. *"Hear … **my righteous plea**"*
      2. Listen. *"Listen to **my cry**"*
      3. Give ear. *"Give ear to **my prayer**" (v 1)*

  B. Vindicate me.

      1. My heart is pure (unmixed motives). *"My prayer … does not rise from deceitful lips" (v 1).*
      2. You alone know that. *"May **my vindication** come from you; may you see **what is right**" (v 2).*

II. The Challenge Of The Pure In Heart.

  A. My Thoughts Are Pure. *"Though you probe **my heart** and examine me at night"*
  B. My Words Are Pure. *"Though you test me, you will find nothing; I have resolved that **my mouth** will not sin" (v 3).*
  C. My Deeds Are Pure. *"As for the deeds of men—by the word of your lips I have kept myself from the ways of the violent. **My steps** have held to your paths; my feet have not slipped" (v 4, 5).*

III. The Confidence Of The Pure In Heart.

  A. You Will Answer Me When I Call. *"I call on you, O God, for **you will** answer me; give ear to me and hear my prayer" (v 6).*
  B. You Will Show Me Your Great Love. *"Show the wonder of **your great love** …"*

C. You Will Save Me by Your Powerful Hand *"… you save by **your right hand** those who take refuge in you from their foes" (v 7).*
D. You Will Keep Me Close; Hide Me Securely. *"Keep me as the apple of your eye; hide me in the shadow of your wings" (v. 8).*

IV. The Concern Of The Pure In Heart.

A. My Enemies Are Out To Get Me! *"… the wicked **assail** me … my enemies **surround** me" (v 9).*

> 1. They are calloused. *"They close up their **callous hearts**"*
> 2. They are arrogant. *"Their mouths speak with **arrogance**" (v 10).*
> 3. They are relentless. *"They have **tracked me down**, they now surround me, with eyes alert, to throw me to the ground" (v 11).*
> 4. They are powerful. *"They are like a lion hungry for prey, **like a great lion** crouching in cover" (v 12).*

B. Unless You Help Me, I Cannot Survive! *"Rise Up, O LORD …"*

> 1. Keep me. *"**Keep me** as the apple of your eye"*
> 2. Hide me. *"**Hide me** in the shadow of your wings"*
> 3. Rescue me. *"Confront them, bring them down; **rescue me** from the wicked by your sword" (v 13).*
> 4. Save me. *"O LORD, by your hand **save me** from such men of this world whose reward is in this life. You still the hunger of those you cherish; their sons have plenty, and they store up wealth for their children" (v 14).*

V. The Consolation of The Pure In Heart.

"And I—in righteousness I will see your face; when I awake, I will be satisfied with seeing your likeness" (v 15).

Psalm 17

The Pure In Heart See God

This psalm is a prayer of supplication by David, a *tephillah* in Hebrew. Only one other psalm, the 86th, carries this superscription. It indicates that the entire psalm is given to prayer. Chiefly, it is a prayer supplicating the Lord for His protection against the accusations of his enemies. As the psalm opens, David imagines himself as a plaintiff in a court of law with God as the judge. He swears, as though under oath, that he is telling the truth, and is innocent of the charge against him. Some have been critical, even shocked, at David's assertions of innocence as though he was suggesting that he was without sin. Maclaren remarks

> "The modern type of religion recoils from such professions (of innocence and purity), and contents itself with always confessing sins which it has given up hope of overcoming, would be all the better for listening to the psalmist and aiming a little more vigorously and hopefully at being able to say, "I know nothing against myself" (I Corinthians 4:4).[Alexander Maclaren, Psalms, Vol. 1, p. 154]

Certainly, he is not saying that he never sins, but that the specific charge against him is false, and he cries out to God, who knows all and sees all, to vindicate him.

He concludes the psalm by saying, *"In righteousness I will see your face."* That reminds us of the sixth beatitude, *"Blessed are the pure in heart, for they will see God" (Matthew 5:8).* Being pure in heart is a good thing, according to Jesus. "Pure" means clean. Its basic meaning is unadulterated, unmixed, unalloyed. A person is pure in heart if he is single in purpose, unconfused in his thinking, and undivided in his will.

With that in mind, let us take a closer look at David's prayer. First we see

The Cry Of The Pure In Heart. *"Hear, O LORD …"*

He entreats the Lord **to listen** to him (to cup His ear), because his prayer comes from a pure heart. In other words, his motives were unmixed. His lips were without deceit. And in view of this, he calls on the Lord **to vindicate** him, to show his cause to be just *"to see what is right."*

Then he issues this remarkable challenge.

The Challenge Of The Pure In Heart.

He asserts that his heart was pure, that he was a man of integrity in his thoughts, his words, and his deeds. In the Sermon on the Mount (Matthew 5), Jesus says that the Beatitude Man is one who lives from the inside out rather than the outside in. He will have integrity in his thoughts, in his words, and in his deeds. That is what characterizes a man of integrity.

In His Thoughts.

*"Though you probe **my heart** and examine me at night."* *(v 3)* You see, Lord, into my innermost being. Nothing can be hidden from your gaze. You see even in the dark. Has your search uncovered anything? That, truly, is a remarkable statement, isn't it?

In His Words.

*"Though you test me, you will find nothing; I have resolved that **my mouth** will not sin."* *(v 3)*. By whatever criteria God or man would use to test him, he is innocent of this charge, whatever it is.

In His Deeds.

*"As for the **deeds** of men—by the word of your lips I have kept myself from the ways of the violent. **My steps** have held to your paths; my feet have not slipped"* *(v 4-5)*.

Next we note

The Confidence Of The Pure In Heart (In His God)

First, he is confident that **the Lord hears him.** *""I call on you, O God, for you will answer me; give ear to me and hear my prayer"* *(v 6)*. Elsewhere he says that the Lord will not hear us if we regard iniquity in our heart, but He delights to answer the prayer of one who sincerely wants to do His will.

Then, he is confident **that the Lord loves him.** ""*Show the wonder of your great love." (v 7)*. That's a good reminder, isn't it? For us who live on this side of the cross, we can say in the awe-hushed tones of the apostle, *"He loved me, and gave himself for me."*

He goes on to speak confidently that **the Lord will save him** by His power-ful hand. *"… you save by your right hand those who take refuge in you from their foes" (v 7)*.

And finally, he expresses confidence that **the Lord would keep him securely close.** *"Keep me as the apple (pupil) of your eye; hide me in the shadow of your wings" (v 8)*. I don't know of anything closer than that, do you? David may have been referring to the wings of the cherubim that covered the very throne of God.

> Under His wings I am safely abiding,
> Though the night deepens and tempests are wild;
> Still I can trust Him—I know He will keep me,
> He has redeemed be and I am His child.
> (William Cushing)

Having assured himself of God's love and care, he proceeds to pour out his heart to God, because he feels surrounded by those who wish to do him harm.

The Concern Of The Pure In Heart.

The description is graphic. He seems to be saying, "My enemies are out to get me." "… *the wicked assail me … my enemies surround me" (v 9)*. And he enlarges on that.

+ They are calloused. *"They close their callous hearts"*
+ They are arrogant. *"Their mouths speak with arrogance" (v 10)*
+ They are relentless. *They have **tracked me down**, they now surround me, with eyes alert, to throw me to the ground" (v 11)*.
+ They are powerful. *They are like a lion hungry for prey, **like a great lion crouching in cover" (v 12)***.

So his cry rings out, *"Rise up, O LORD …"* Unless you come to my rescue, I cannot survive! Keep me, hide me, rescue me, save me! It sounds like Peter sinking beneath the waves. *"Lord, save me!"* These were real, tangible enemies that David faced. Ours are not always that tangible, but no less real. Paul tells us that unseen enemies bent on our destruction surround us. But the panoply of God is there for us, if we will put it on (Ephesians 6).

Assured of the Lord's timely intervention, David is comforted.

The Consolation Of The Pure In Heart.

"And I—in righteousness I will see your face; when I awake, I will be satisfied with seeing your likeness" (v 15).

Some see in this a reference to resurrection: his awaking from death to see the face of God. More likely, David is saying that when he feels surrounded by his enemies, he feels even more surrounded by the protecting arms of God, and his restless heart finds peace in the Lord's presence.

> *Lord, it is comforting to know that you have promised to be with us always, never leaving us or forsaking us. David reminds us of your constant love and faithfulness. Even more than David experienced, we are brought so close to you because of Jesus that we cannot get any nearer. We desire to live before you with pure hearts that desire only and always to do your blessed will.*

Things To Ponder

John said that no one has seen God, but Jesus (the Living Word) came to declare Him or manifest Him. Certainly, He is also "seen" in His Word, the written Word. God wants us to "see" Him and "know" Him, and has gone to great lengths to reveal Himself to us. By the way, Psalm 19 that we shall look at shortly tells us that we can also know Him through His Creative Word.

Psalm 18

"The King Victorious"

Psalm 18

For the director of music (choirmaster).
Of David the servant of the LORD.

He sang to the LORD the words of this song when the LORD delivered him
from the hand of all his enemies and from the hand of Saul. He said:

1 I love you, O LORD, my strength.

2 The LORD is my rock, my fortress and my deliverer;
    My God is my rock, in whom I take refuge.
    He is my shield and the horn of my salvation, my stronghold.
3 I call to the LORD, who is worthy of praise,
    and I am saved from my enemies.

4 The cords of death entangled me;
    the torrents of destruction overwhelmed me.
5 The cords of the grave coiled around me;
    the snares of death confronted me.
6 In my distress I called to the LORD; I cried to my God for help.
    From his temple he heard my voice;
    my cry came before him, into his ears.

7 The earth trembled and quaked,
    and the foundations of the mountains shook;
    they trembled because he was angry.
8 Smoke rose from his nostrils;
    consuming fire came from his mouth,
    burning coals blazed out of it.
9 He parted the heavens and came down;
    dark clouds were under his feet.
10 He mounted the cherubim and flew;
    he soared on the wings of the wind.
11 He made darkness his covering,
    his canopy around him—the dark rain clouds of the sky.

12 Out of the brightness of his presence clouds advanced,
     with hailstones and bolts of lightning.
13 The LORD thundered from heaven;
     the voice of the Most High resounded.
14 He shot his arrows and scattered the enemies,
     great bolts of lightning and routed them.
15 The valleys of the sea were exposed
     and the foundations of the earth laid bare at your rebuke,
O LORD, at the blast of breath from your nostrils.

16 He reached down from on high and took hold of me;
     he drew me out of deep waters.
17 He rescued me from my powerful enemy,
     from my foes, who were too strong for me.
18 They confronted me in the day of my disaster,
     but the LORD was my support.
19 He brought me out into a spacious place;
     he rescued me because he delighted in me.

20 The LORD has dealt with me according to my righteousness; according to
     the cleanness of my hands he has rewarded me.
21 For I have kept the ways of the LORD;
     I have not done evil by turning from my God.
22 All his laws are before me; I have not turned away from his decrees.
23 I have been blameless before him
     and have kept myself from sin.
24 The LORD has rewarded me according to my righteousness, according to
     the cleanness of my hands in his sight.

25 To the faithful you show yourself faithful,
     to the blameless you show yourself blameless,
26 to the pure you show yourself pure,
     but to the crooked you show yourself shrewd.
27 You save the humble but bring low those whose eyes are haughty.
28 You, O LORD, keep my lamp burning;
     my God turns my darkness into light.
29 With your help I can advance against a troop;
     with my God I can scale a wall.

30 As for God, his way is perfect;
    the word of the LORD is flawless.
    He is a shield for all who take refuge in him.

31 For who is God besides the LORD?
    And who is the Rock except our God?
32 It is God who arms me with strength
    and makes my way perfect.
33 He makes my feet like the feet of a deer;
    he enables me He trains my hands for battle;
    my arms can bend a bow of bronze.
35 You give me your shield of victory,
    and your right hand sustains me;
    you stoop down to make me great.
36 You broaden the path beneath me,
    so that my ankles do not turn.
37 I pursued my enemies and overtook them;
    I did not turn back till they were destroyed.
38 I crushed them so that they could not rise;
    they fell beneath my feet.
39 You armed me with strength for battle;
    you made my adversaries bow at my feet.
40 You made my enemies turn their backs in flight,
    and I destroyed my foes.
41 They cried for help, but there was no one to save them to the LORD, but he
    did not answer.
42 I beat them as fine as dust borne on the wind;
    I poured them out like mud in the streets.
43 You have delivered me from the attacks of the people;
    you have made me the head of nations;
    people I did not know are subject to me.
44 As soon as they hear me, they obey me;
    foreigners cringe before me.
45 They all lose heart; they come trembling from their strongholds.

46 The LORD lives! Praise be to my Rock!
    Exalted be God my Savior!

47 He is the God who avenges me,
　　who subdues nations under me,
　　You exalted me above my foes;
　　from violent men you rescued me.
49 Therefore I will praise you among the nations, O LORD;
　　I will sing praises to your name.
50 He gives his king great victories;
　　he shows unfailing kindness to his anointed,
　　to David and his descendants forever.

NIV

Psalm 18

The Victorious Warrior King

The occasion for this psalm as given in the heading is David's deliverance from the hand of his enemies and from the hand of Saul. The historical note is 2 Samuel 22:1. He responds with a threefold pledge to God the Mighty Deliverer.

I. The Refuge: I Will Love You, O LORD—For When I Am In Trouble, You Are My Refuge (v 1-2).

"I love you, O Lord, my strength ..."

> A. My Strength—for all my weakness.
> B. My Rock—where I find stability.
> C. My Fortress—where I find security.
> D. My Deliverer—who rescues me from the hand of the enemy.
> E. My Shield—behind whom I find protection.
> F. My Horn of Salvation—where my enemies cannot touch me.
> G. My Stronghold—where no foe can enter.

II. The Rescue: I Will Call On You, LORD—For When My Enemies Overwhelm Me, You Hear And Answer Me, And Come To My Rescue . (v 3-19).

*"**I call** to the Lord, who is worthy of praise, and I am saved from my enemies" (v 3) "In my distress **I called** to the Lord; **I cried** to my God for help. From his temple he heard my voice; my cry came before him, into his ears"(v 6).*

> A. Death and destruction entangle and overwhelm me. I cry out in my distress and he hears and answers me (v 4-5).
> B. I mean—he really answers me!
>
> > 1. How? He comes swiftly, like an ominous approaching storm that darkens, rumbles, lights up the sky, and finally unleashes its fury (v 7-15).
> > 2. When? Just in time, He reaches down and draws me up and out of deep waters, rescuing me from my powerful foes (v 16-18). God's marvelous display of power was for the purpose of rescuing His servant.

3. Why? Because he delighted in me and desires to reward me (v 19-20)

   + I have lived righteously—with clean hands (v 20, 24).
   + I have lived obediently—keeping his ways, obeying his laws (v 21-22)
   + I have lived blamelessly—keeping myself from sin (v 23)

4. What? What is His method of operation? God does what He does because of Who He is. He responds to the responsive!

   + To the faithful he shows himself faithful.
   + To the blameless he shows himself blameless (v 25)
   + To the pure he shows himself pure.
   + To the crooked (savage) he shows himself shrewd (v 26).
   "those who plot against you are plotted against"
   + He lifts up the humble, and brings low the proud (v 27).

D. This God is my God! (v 29-32)

   1. *"with my God"*—I am invincible!
   2. *"As for God"*—He is perfect in every way
   3. *"Who is God"*—He is incomparable!
   4. *"It is God"*—He is unbeatable!

   He arms me (v 32)
   He makes me (v 33)
   He enables me (v 33)
   He trains me (v 34)
   He sustains me (v 35)
   He exalts me (v 35)
   He helps me (v 36)
   He fights for me (v 37)
   He delivers me (v 43)

E. Therefore, all my enemies are defeated!

   They are utterly defeated (v 37).
   They are crushed beneath my feet (v 38).
   They bow at my feet (v 39).
   They flee in terror before me. (v 40).

They cry but there is no answer. (v 41).
They are beaten down and poured out (v 42).
They are subject to me and cringe before me (v 43-45)
They all lose heart, and come trembling before me (v 46).

III. The Response: I Will Give Thanks To You, O LORD—For You Have Shown Me Great Kindness (v 46-50). *"The LORD lives! Praise be to my Rock! Exalted be God my Savior! (v 46) "Therefore I will give thanks to you among the nations, O LORD; I will sing praises to your name" (v 49).*

A. I will praise you, my Rock and my Savior!

1. You avenge me (v 47)
2. You subdue nations before me (v 47).
3. You save me (v 48).
4. You exalt me (v 48).
5. You rescue me (v 48).

B. I will praise you among the nations!

1. You give great victories to me (v 50).
2. You show unfailing kindness to me (v 50).
3. To me, David, and to my descendants forever! (v 50).

Psalm 18

The Victorious Warrior King

This delightful psalm is somewhat long, but rewards the careful reader eager to catch a vision of God through the eyes of the psalmist. The occasion for the psalm is immediately apparent in the heading. It is David's response to God's deliverance from the hand of his enemies, and particularly Saul, the reigning king. The entire psalm is found in its historical setting in 2 Samuel 22, and the occasion in verse 1 matches the occasion given here.

> *"David sang to the Lord the words of this song when the Lord delivered him from the hand of all his enemies and from the hand of Saul"*

The subject matter of the psalm could be divided into three parts corresponding to the deliverance from his enemies, and the threefold pledge David offers to God.

1. The Refuge. He says, "I will love you, O LORD", for when I am in trouble, you are my refuge (v 1-2).

2. The Rescue. He says, "I will call on you, LORD", for when my enemies overwhelm me, you hear and answer me, and come swiftly to my rescue.

3. The Response. He says, "I will give thanks to you, O LORD", for you have shown me great kindness (v 46-50).

Let's look at it more carefully.

The Refuge. "I Will Love You, O LORD" (v 1-2)

David brings before us one of the most extensive lists recorded in the Word that underscore the truth that the Lord is there for us when we face situations too overwhelming for us; when we are in great danger and distress. They are seven ways of saying essentially the same thing. He is my Strength for all my weakness. (Paul says essentially the same thing in 2 Corinthians 12:9, 10, *"My grace is sufficient for you, for my strength is made perfect in weakness … For when I am weak, then I am strong."*)

1. He is my Rock in whom I take refuge.

2. He is my Fortress in whom I find security.

3. He is my Shield behind which I shelter.

4. He is my Deliverer who rescues me from my enemies.

5. He is my Horn of Salvation where no enemy can touch me.

6. He is my Stronghold where no foe may enter.

The theme is repeated over and over in the psalms. *"God is our refuge and strength, a very present help in trouble" (Psalm 46:1).*

The Rescue. "I Will Call On You, LORD" (v 3-19)

Because David knows his God, he is emboldened to come to Him and *"find grace to help in time of need."* Another great theme throughout the psalms is "I called ... he answered." Hear him say, *"I call to the Lord, who is worthy of praise, and I am saved from my enemies" (v 3). "In my distress I called to the Lord; I cried to my God for help. From his temple he heard my voice; my cry came before him, into his ears" (v 6).* David was sure that the moment he voiced his request, God bent down and cupped his ear to hear what he had to say. Isn't that a great view of prayer! God doesn't ignore the petitioner. He doesn't turn a deaf ear to his plea. He listens, and in the case of the psalmist, he springs into action.

Death and destruction entangle and overwhelm him. He cries out in his distress and God hears and answers!

> *"The cords of death **entangled** me; the torrents of destruction **overwhelmed** me. The cords of the grave **coiled** around me; the snares of death **confronted** me. In my **distress** I called to the LORD; I cried to my God for help. From his temple he heard my voice; my cry came before him, into his ears" (v 3-6).*

The letters in bold type certainly leave us in no doubt that David's back was against the wall; that he was overwhelmed, and needed help without delay.

He seems to say in the verses that follow that God not only answered him, but also **really** answered him. He wants to dramatize God's response. God was in no way apathetic to his plight, or casual in his reaction to his request.

How did He answer? He came swiftly, like an ominous approaching storm that darkens, rumbles, lights up the sky, and finally unleashes its fury on the landscape! Notice how he graphically describes God's response to his request. God came angrily, speedily, and powerfully!

> *"The earth trembled and quaked, and the foundations of the mountains shook; they trembled because he was angry. Smoke rose from his nostrils; consuming fire came from his mouth, burning coals blazed out of it. He parted the heavens and came down; dark clouds were under his feet. He mounted the cherubim and flew; he soared on the wings of the wind. He made darkness his covering, his canopy around him—the dark rain clouds of the sky. Out of the brightness of his presence clouds advanced, with hailstones and bolts of lightning. The LORD thundered from heaven; the voice of the Most High resounded. He shoots his arrows and scattered [the enemies], great bolts of lightning and routed them. The valleys of the sea were exposed and the foundations of the earth laid bare at your rebuke, O LORD, at the blast of breath from your nostrils" (v 7-15).*

Isn't that a great description? David is saying, "You talk about an answer. Now that's an answer—unmistakable, powerful, and dramatic!

When did God answer? Just in the nick of time. God swooped down from the sky, took hold of David, and lifted him out of his deep trouble.

> *"He reached down from on high and took hold of me; he drew me out of deep waters. He rescued me from my powerful enemy, from my foes, who were too strong for me. They confronted me in the day of my disaster, but the Lord was my support. He brought me out into a spacious place; he rescued me because he delighted in me" (v 16-19).*

God did more than David expected. He rescued him, and *"brought him out into a **spacious** (broad) place."* This stands over against the straitened place where he had been. As the apostle put it, *"He is able to do exceedingly, abundantly, above all that we ask or think" (Ephesians 3:20).*

And why would God do that for him? David reflects on that, and his answer may trouble us a bit since we are so conditioned to believe that God acts toward us "in spite of" rather that "because of." That's what grace is, right? David and God were covenant partners. David is affirming that God delights in him, is pleased with him, when he is obeying His word, following His way, and living in a way that would glorify Him. All the rewards for living a godly life are not reserved alone for the afterlife.

"The Lord has dealt with me according to my righteousness; according to the cleanness of my hands he has rewarded me. For I have kept the ways of the Lord; I have not done evil by turning from my God. All his laws are before me; I have not turned away from his decrees. I have been blameless before him and have kept myself from sin. The LORD has answered me according to my righteousness, according to the cleanness of my hands in his sight" (v 20-24).

As children of God, we need to remember that although we are not saved because of our righteousness, God is pleased when we live righteous lives. Paul tells us that in Christ we are "declared righteous" by God. He imputes to us the very righteousness of Christ. Now, Paul says, we who "are righteous" need to "be righteous" even as He is righteous. It pleases God when we are obedient! It is the way we show our love for Him. It is exciting that God delights in us; that we can give him pleasure. It was said of righteous Enoch *"before his translation he had this testimony, **that he pleased God." (Hebrews 13:5).***

In fact, David says, this is God's normal method of operation. He responds to the responsive! To the faithful he shows himself faithful. To the blameless he shows himself blameless. To the pure he shows himself pure. But to the crooked he shows himself shrewd. Someone has translated that "those who plot against you, you plot against." Another principle of God's dealing is given in verse 27, *"He lifts up the humble, and brings low the proud."*

And David exclaims, *"This God is my God!"* He mentions God four times in verses 29-32.

1. *"My God"*—*"You, O LORD, keep my lamp burning; **my God** turns my darkness into light. With your help I can advance against a troop; with **my God** I can scale a wall."(v 27-28)* He is saying that His God not only goes before Him, illuminating His way, but goes with Him, enabling him to do what otherwise would be impossible and unthinkable.

2. *"As for God"*—everything God reveals is perfect; everything God says is perfect; everything God does is perfect. *"As for God, his way is perfect; the word of the LORD is flawless. He is a shield for all who take refuge in him"* (v 30). In other words, God can be counted on!

3. *"Who is God"*—He is incomparable. *"For who is God besides the LORD? And who is the Rock except our God?"(v 31).*

4.*"It is God"*—He makes me unbeatable! Notice the things God does for David that makes him the victorious warrior. Note that the battle is swift and decisive, because it is God who fights with him and for him.

He arms me. *"It is God who arms me with strength and makes my way perfect"* *(v 32).*

He enables me. *"He makes my feet like the feet of a deer; he enables me to stand on the heights"* *(v 33).*

He trains (equips) me. *"He trains my hands for battle; my arms can bend a bow of bronze"* *(v 34).*

He sustains me. *"You give me your shield of victory, and your right hand sustains me"* *(v 35).*

He exalts me. *"You stoop down to make me great"* *(v 35).* (What an interesting picture of God!)

He helps me. *"You broaden the path beneath me, so that my ankles do not turn."* *(v 36)*

He fights for me. *"I pursued my enemies and overtook them; I did not turn back till they were destroyed"* *(v 37).*

He delivers me. *"You have delivered me from the attacks of the people; you have made me the head of nations; people I did not know are subject to me"* *(v 43).*

The deliverance is now complete. His enemies are completely vanquished, utterly defeated. This he elaborates in verses 37-46. I will simply list his description of his victories. Read these verses for the full effect.

They are utterly defeated (v 37)
They are crushed beneath my feet (v 28).
They bow at my feet (v 39).
The flee in terror before me (v 40.
They cry out, but there is no answer (v 41).
They are beaten down and poured out (v 42).
They are subject to me and cringe before me (v 43-45).
They all lose heart, and come trembling before me (v 46)

This brings him quite naturally to the grateful response.

The Response. "I Will Give Thanks To You, O LORD"

He says, *"I will praise you, my Rock and my Savior!"* He briefly summarizes what God had done for him in verses 47-48).

You avenge me.
You subdue nations before me.
You save me.

You exalt me.
You rescue me.

Finally, David, in verses 49 and 50, offers thanks to God "among the nations." It is interesting that Paul, in Romans 15:9, quotes from verse 49 here as he exhorts the Gentiles to glorify God for His great mercy in extending the gospel to them. *"I will praise you among the nations, O LORD; I will sing praises to your name."*

David's concluding statement is *"He gives his king great victories; he shows unfailing kindness to his anointed, to David, and his descendants forever."* The "forever" reminds us of God's covenant with David. A greater Son of David will yet sit on his throne, and His dominion will be forever and ever.

> *Our Father, we give you thanks for this psalm for it reveals you once again as the God who is there for us, your people. It reminds us again of your attentiveness to our prayers, and your sensitivity to our needs. Help us to give you pleasure by our loving obedience. Teach us that life works for us when we go your way, and works against us when we pursue our own way. Like David, we must learn to humbly depend on you, for without you we are nothing and can do nothing, but with you we can do what ordinarily we could not do. When we face life together, we are an unbeatable team! Thank you, our Rock and our Redeemer!*

Things to Ponder

1. Take a few moments to meditate on the seven symbols David gives that speak of God's strength, stability, and security.

2. Have you found the affirmation of David true for you when he said, *"I called ... He answered?"*

3. God is a responsive and loving Person. Why should we find it strange that as we respond to Him, He responds to us? Jesus said, *"If anyone loves me, he will obey my teaching. My Father will love him, and we will come to him and make our home with him"* (John 14:23).

Psalm 19

"God is Speaking. Listen!"

Psalm 19

For the director of music.

A psalm of David.

1 The heavens declare the glory of God;
    the skies proclaim the work of his hands.
2 Day after day they pour forth speech;
    night after night they display knowledge.
3 There is no speech or language where their voice is not heard.
4 Their voice goes out into all the earth,
    their words to the ends of the world.
    In the heavens he has pitched a tent for the sun,
5 which is like a bridegroom coming forth from his pavilion,
    like a champion rejoicing to run his course.
6 It rises at one end of the heavens and makes its circuit to the other;
    nothing is hidden from its heat.

7 The law of the LORD is perfect,
    reviving the soul.
    The statutes of the LORD are trustworthy,
    making wise the simple.
8 The precepts of the LORD are right,
    giving joy to the heart.
    The commands of the LORD are radiant,
    giving light to the eyes.
9 The fear of the LORD is pure,
    enduring forever.
    The ordinances of the LORD are sure
    and altogether righteous.

10 They are more precious than gold, than much pure gold;
    they are sweeter than honey, than honey from the comb.
11 By them is your servant warned;
    in keeping them there is great reward.

12 Who can discern his errors?
    Forgive my hidden faults.
13 Keep your servant also from willful sins;
    may they not rule over me.
    Then will I be blameless, innocent of great transgression.

14 May the words of my mouth and the meditation of my heart
    be pleasing in your sight,
    O LORD, my Rock and my Redeemer.

NIV

Psalm 19

God Is Speaking—Listen!

I. God's Witness In The Skies. His Works

His Natural Revelation—Declares His Glory.

"The heavens declare the glory of God; the skies proclaim the work of his hands" (v. 1).

A. A specific witness. *"… are telling … are declaring" (v 1).*
B. An incessant witness. *"day after day … night after night" (v 2).*
C. An inaudible witness. *"… no speech or language … nor voice" (v 3).*
D. A universal witness. *"… into all the earth … to the ends of the world" (v 4).*
E. A glorious witness. *"… the sun … like a bridegroom. like a champion" (v 5)*

+ *coming forth*
+ *rejoicing to run his course*
+ *rises at one end*
+ *makes its circuit to the other*
+ *nothing hidden from its heat*

II. God's Witness In The Scriptures. His Word.

His Special Revelation—Reveals His Greatness.

A. God's Word Described (What it is called)

1. Law.
2. Statutes.
3. Precepts.
4. Commands.
5. Awe Inspiring (Fear or Reverence).
6. Ordinances.

B. God's Word Detailed. (What it is)

1. Perfect … complete, nothing lacking
2. Trustworthy … sure, warranting our fullest confidence
3. Right … clearly showing the correct way
4. Radiant … a lamp to our feet, a light to our path
5. Pure … clear, understandable, unambiguous
6. True … real, showing things as they really are and are meant to be

C. God's Word Demonstrated. (What it does)

1. Revives the soul.
2. Makes wise the simple.
3. Gives joy to the heart.
4. Gives light to the eyes.
5. Endures forever.
6. Vindicated or Righteous all together

D. God's Word Compared. (What it's like)

1. Like gold *"more precious than gold, than much pure (fine) gold" (v 10)*

    + precious
    + priceless

2. Like honey *"sweeter than honey, than honey from the comb" (v 10)*

    + palatable
    + pleasing

III. God's Witness In The Soul. His Will.

His Practical Revelation—Shows His Grace.

A. Response of the Soul to the Word.

1. Warned. *"By them is your servant warned …"*
2. Rewarded. *"… in keeping them there is great reward" (v 11).*

B. Realization in the Soul of the Word.

"Who can discern his errors? Forgive my hidden faults. Keep your servant also from willful sins; may they not rule over me. Then will I be blameless, innocent of great transgression" (v 11-13).

1. God's Word points out my errors and mistakes.
2. God's Word reveals and offers forgiveness for faults of which I am unaware.
3. God's Word enables me to keep from willful sins so that they do not rule over me.
4. God's Word keeps me blameless and innocent from flagrant transgression.

C. Request of the Soul To The Lord … His Rock and Redeemer

1. *"May the **words of my mouth** be acceptable to You."*
2. *"May the **meditations of my heart** be pleasing in Your sight". (v 14).*

Psalm 19

God Is Speaking—Listen!

Does the God who made us want us to know him? I mean know him intimately—personal and up close. The Bible answers affirmatively. In fact, God has gone to great lengths to make himself known to man. At least three aspects of revelation are to be discerned in Scripture:

The *cosmos*, that is, God's general and natural revelation to man in the world that he has made. Eli-God (used once in these first six verses), is the *"Maker of heaven and earth."*

The *nomos*, that is, God's written word, his special revelation, that gives to man a more particular and detailed understanding of His purpose and will.

The *logos*, that is, the Living Word, manifested through his incarnate Son who came to reveal to man the glory of the Father. This latter revelation is the fullest, the most complete, unfolding of himself God will give to us. The author of Hebrews says emphatically that there will be no further revelation.

> *In the past God spoke to our forefathers through the prophets at many times and in various ways,* **but in these last days he has spoken to us by his Son,** *whom he appointed heir of all things, and through whom he made the universe. The Son is the radiance of God's glory and the exact representation of his being, sustaining all things by his powerful word. After he had provided purification for sins, he sat down at the right hand of the majesty in heaven"* (Hebrews 1:1-4).

God reveals Himself, therefore, in His World and in His Word. In natural revelation God speaks, but inaudibly. It is visible yet silent, but still powerful. I like G. Campbell Morgan's description "the speech of a great silence." Although the witness is silent, there is a sense in which it speaks eloquently to anyone with a heart to listen.

In special revelation Yahweh (used seven times) speaks audibly, and His words have been delivered to and transcribed by men. This revelation was given in history and embodied in Scripture. It details God's plan of redemption—from eternity to eternity.

Here in Psalm 19, David first deals with natural revelation. Theologians call it general revelation because everyone receives it. In Romans 1:18ff. God's self-revelation in nature becomes the basis for Paul's indictment of the whole pagan world as without excuse, sinful and guilty before God. In their rebellion against God, they worship the Creature (the essence of worldliness) rather than the Creator . The apostle puts it this way,

"The wrath of God is being revealed from heaven against all the godlessness and wickedness of men who suppress the truth by their wickedness, since what can be known about God is plain to them, because God has made it plain to them. For since the creation of the world God's invisible qualities—his eternal power and divine nature—have been clearly seen, being understood from what has been made, so that men are without excuse" (Romans 1:19-20.

So in this psalm David says that God exists. God has revealed Himself, and does reveal Himself. He is speaking. Man must listen!

Consider first of all,

God's Witness In The Skies—His Works. *"The heavens declare the glory of God; the skies proclaim the work of his hands" (v 1).*

The psalmist tells us the *what* and the *how* of God's revelation.

The *what* is seen in the opening statement, *"The heavens declare the glory of God."* God created the heavens and they declare His glory. A personal and powerful God brought everything into existence. The Bible begins with the simple statement, *"In the beginning God created …"* It does not elaborate, but assumes this to be the simple truth that explains the origin of the universe, and all that is in it. God originates and man speculates. The word *firmament,* in some translations, is just a Hebrew parallelism to "heavens." Genesis 1:6 calls this expanse "sky."

This second phrase tells us *how* God created. It was all the result of God's handiwork. Psalm 8 calls it God's "finger" work. These are poetic descriptions of God's powerful working. The author of Hebrews suggests that God simply spoke a word of command, and the vast universe was formed out of nothing (Hebrews 11:3).

Notice the description of this witness in the skies. It is specific, incessant, inaudible, universal, and glorious.

1. It is a specific witness. *"The heavens declare … the skies proclaim" (v 1)* It is a witness with content and meaning.

2. It is an incessant witness. *"Day after day … night after night" (v 2).* The witness never ceases. They roll on, march on, without interruption. The two balance each other for without the night, the sky seems empty. Each has a witness unique to it.

3. It is an inaudible witness. Lit. *"No speech, no language, no voice is heard" (v 3)*. Kidner calls it "the paradox of wordless speech."

4. It is a universal witness. *"Their voice (line) goes out into all the earth, their words to the ends of the world" (v 4)*. Kidner further suggests that the translation "line" could mean that there are no boundaries that restrict the witness, although "cry" is probably to be preferred.

And finally, David brings the sun into focus, suggesting that …

5. It is a glorious witness. *"In the heavens He has pitched a tent for the sun, which is like a bridegroom coming forth from his pavilion, like a champion rejoicing to run his course. It rises at one end of the heavens and makes its circuit to the other; nothing is hidden from its heat" (v 5-6)*. The psalmist uses two figures of speech here to describe the sun—a bridegroom and a runner (someone has suggested a soldier rather than runner). The idea is that the sun has a particular role to play in God's order of things, and does not deviate from that declared purpose. The sun in all its brilliance and glory is there, but the God who created it and orders it shines brighter in His glory.

Next David speaks of the revelation of God in His Word.

God's Witness In The Scriptures—His Word.

Here we see Hebrew parallelism in the psalms at its best. The nouns, adjectives, and verbs provide a simple outline for our examination of the text.

God's Word Is Described. What it's called? These nouns are all somewhat synonymous in meaning, but "have a certain character of their own" (Kidner).

1. Law. The Torah—Yahweh's revelation for the purpose of instruction and teaching concerning His will. God does not leave us ignorant as to what He wants us to do.

2. Statutes or Testimony. These are not just any words. They are God's words, and He witnesses to their veracity. They are Yahweh's covenant-declarations to His people.

3. Precepts. These are precise teachings or rules of moral conduct

4. Commandments. Commandments are imperatives and are not addressed to the intellect but to the will. One cannot simply believe a command; it must be obeyed.

5. **Awe-Inspiring.** This shows the kind of reverent response appropriate to recipients.

6. **Ordinances. Judgments.** Our relationships must be consistent with justice.

God's Word is Detailed. What it is. These adjectives declare that God's Word is sufficient for all of life.

1. **Perfect.** It is complete. There is nothing lacking. Paul says in 2 Timothy 3:16 and 17 that the God-breathed Scriptures are *"useful for teaching, rebuking, correcting and training in righteousness so that the man of God may be thoroughly equipped for every good work."*

2. **Trustworthy (Sure).** God's word is firm as well as confirmed—verified (Kidner). It is certain, reliable, and warrants our fullest confidence.

3. **Right.** It is what the proverb means when it says that if we trust God with all our heart, and not lean to our own understanding, He will "make our paths straight." (Proverbs 3:5, 6) The right (righteous) way is always the best way!

4. **Radiant (Pure).** God's word throws its light on our pathway to show us the way. Only God's word can bring understanding and comfort to the heart in the deep and dark times of life.

5. **Clean.** It is relevant and constant amid the change and decay of our age. It will outlast time.

6. **True.** The word of God is real, showing things as they really are and things as they ought to be. To know the truth, Jesus says, is to be free.

God's Word is Demonstrated. (What it does) These verbs show the powerful effect the Word of God has in the human soul.

1. **It revives the soul.** *"He restores my soul"* (Psalm 23:3).

2. **It makes wise the simple.** It enables a simple, unlearned person, to be wise!

3. **It gives joy to the heart.** Joy comes when we are obedient to God's word. Contrary to popular belief, God wants us to be happy.

4. **It gives light to the eyes.** God's word is a preventative. It keeps us from stumbling.

5. **It is all together righteous.** There is no distortion of truth here. It is absolutely reliable.

God's Word Is Compared. (What It's Like) Two similies are used:

> 1. **It's like gold—priceless, precious.** *"more precious than gold, than much pure (fine)gold"*
> 2. **It's like honey—palatable and pleasing.** *"sweeter than honey, than honey from the comb"*

How precious and pleasing is the Word of God to you?

The psalmist concludes by pointing to the practical benefits in the soul of obedience to the Word of God.

God's Witness In The Soul—His Will. Could we call it practical revelation?

First, there is **the response of the soul to the Word.** *"By them is your servant warned; in keeping them there is great reward" (v 11).* Warned and rewarded. One is negative, and the other positive. The warnings are inevitable. The double—edged sword of the Word penetrates into our very being. Everything is laid bare, uncovered to God's searching gaze (Hebrews 4:12-13). But the wealth is incalculable. New treasures are uncovered every day as we obediently discover His will.

Second, there is **the realization in the soul of the Word.** *"Who can discern his errors? Forgive my hidden faults. Keep your servant also from willful sins; may they not rule over me. Then will I be blameless, innocent of great transgression" (v 11-13).*

What does God word do?

1. It points out my errors and mistakes.
2. It reveals and offers forgiveness for faults of which I am unaware.
3. It enables me to keep from willful sins so that they do not rule over me.
4. It keeps me blameless and innocent from flagrant transgressions.

And finally, there is **the request of the soul to Yahweh, His Rock and Redeemer.** *"May the words of my mouth be acceptable to You. May the meditations of my heart be pleasing in Your sight" (v 14).* Accept the offerings of praise from my lips and from my life. What a wonderful way to end this lovely psalm!

This psalm, Lord, tells me in no uncertain terms that you want to be known, have made yourself known to us. You have revealed yourself in the creative Word, and the written Word, but supremely in the Living Word. Your Son, our Savior and Lord. Oh help us to listen closely to what you are trying to tell us. Open our

eyes to see and our ears to hear! Help us to see that creation is one vast window
through which we can see your majesty and glory.

Things To Ponder

Are the words of our lips and the thoughts of our heart acceptable and pleasing to God?

Psalm 20

"Lord, Save The King!"

Psalm 20

For the director of music.

A psalm of David.

1 May the LORD answer you when you are in distress;
    may the name of the God of Jacob protect you.

2 May he send you help from the sanctuary and
    grant you support from Zion.

3 May he remember all your sacrifices and
    accept your burnt offerings. Selah

4 May he give you the desire of your heart
    and make all your plans succeed.

5 We will shout for joy when you are victorious
    and will lift up our banners in the name of our God.
    May the LORD grant all your requests.

6 Now I know that the LORD saves his anointed;
    he answers him from his holy heaven with
    the saving power of his right hand.

7 Some trust in chariots and some in horses,
    but we trust in the name of the LORD our God.

8 They are brought to their knees and fall,
    but we rise up and stand firm.

9 O LORD, **save the king!**
    Answer us when we call!

NIV

Psalm 20

Our Prayers Go With You

The psalm falls into three natural divisions:

I. The People's Prayer For Their King.

A. The Person who goes with you. *"The Lord answer you in the day of trouble! The name of the God of Jacob protect you!" (v 1)*
B. The power that will strengthen you. *"May he send you help from the sanctuary, and give you support from Zion (v 2)*
C. The provision that sustains you. *"May you remember all your offerings, and regard with favor your burnt offerings."(v 3)*
D. The promise that satisfies you. *"May he grant you your heart's desire, and fulfill all your plans." (v 4)*

II. The Response Of the King.

A. The anticipation of victory. *"Now I know that the Lord saves his anointed; he answers from his holy heaven with the saving power of his right hand." (v 6).*
B. He knows where his victory lies. *"Some trust in chariots and some in horses, but we trust in the name of the LORD our God" (v 7)*

III. The Benediction. *"Give victory to (save) the king, O Lord; answer us when we call" (v 9)*

Psalm 20

Our Prayers Go With you

A few years ago, one of our young people, in the church I served for many years, was going on a mission to South America, specifically the country of Argentina, to teach in a school for missionary children. I was searching for a text of Scripture to encourage her on the Sunday she was commissioned. At the same time I wanted to challenge the people of the church family to "hold the ropes" for her in prayer. I found the passage I was looking for here in Psalm 20.

Actually, this lovely Psalm is the song that the people of Israel sang when the king went forth to battle. Before he went out to face the peril and uncertainty of war, they sang this psalm as a prayer for his safety and victory. It certainly wasn't just a nice custom to be observed. It was a genuine prayer expressing their faith, their trust in the power of the living God who would keep the king and his armies in the midst of desperate battle.

I reminded our people that morning that God has made every believer in Jesus Christ both a king and a priest? So we are justified, I believe, when we read Old Testament stories about kings and priests, to apply these truths to ourselves. They are designed to teach us how a king ought to act and how a priest ought to behave, to lead us through experiences that kings and priests have, and to show us the way. The battle is joined; the forces of the evil one are largely in control in our world. Ours is a spiritual warfare that won't quit until our conquering king returns to rule and reign. Paul reminds us *our struggle is not against flesh and blood, but against the rulers, against the authorities, against the powers of this dark world and against the spiritual forces of evil in the heavenly realms. Therefore put on the full armor of God" (Eph. 6:12,13).*

Make no mistake about it. Our enterprising and youthful teacher would have to engage those forces during the year ahead. Into her care would be entrusted the precious lives of our missionary children. These are formative years, important years. Satan would delight to destroy the peace of mind and effectiveness of the missionary parents through the children if he could. We renewed our commitment to pray for the dorm-parents of those children whom our church had supported for many years. What a tremendous responsibility is theirs to stand-in for the parents in the training of their children. We prayed that this team of workers would be committed in love to the Lord first, then to each other, and then to these children, that the year might be a year of real growth for all concerned.

So we as priests pledged ourselves to carry on a ministry of intercession for our king, or should I say queen, as she went out to engage the enemy. Perhaps this ancient prayer might offer some guidelines for us as we intercede for others in their ministry opportunities.

The psalm falls into three natural divisions. The first five verses are the people's prayer for the king. In verses 6 through 8 we have the king's response. Verse 9 is a shout of benediction by the people.

The People's Prayer For Their King

The Person Who Goes With You

Our first request concerns **the Person that goes with you.** *"The Lord answer you in the day of trouble! The name of the God of Jacob protect you!"*

Right at the start there is the recognition that trouble lies ahead for you. It is not easy to fight battles. But the way that you are going to find your way through is carefully spelled out here. Your refuge lies in the Lord—in the name of the God of Jacob. Only He is adequate for the situation. Only he can tell what dangers lay ahead. Only He has the insight and wisdom to steer your course aright. If you do not trust and rest upon the God of Jacob, you will never make it.

Why does he say *"the God of Jacob?"* Elsewhere (in Psalm 46) the psalmist declares, *"The Lord of hosts is with us; the God of Jacob is our stronghold."* The word "hosts" might refer to the starry heavens, or the angelic messengers, or the people of God, but it declares that the God of stars, seraphims, and saints is the God of one little man, Jacob, by name. Jacob is the maneuverer, the manipulator, the wheeler-dealer, and the big-time operator. He always had a plan in mind that seemed to always contradict God's purpose for his life. He depended upon his wits, his wisdom, and his wiles to accomplish what he wanted. But God finally got through to Jacob, and Hebrews 11 lists him as one of the hero of faith, because he finally learned to lean on the top of his staff and worship. That is why God is called here *"the God of Jacob."*

When you face trouble, don't panic. Don't cast about for some kind of maneuver to accomplish what you want. Let God be the God of Jacob—let him be with you and for you a refuge.

The Power That Will Strengthen You

Our second request concerns the Power that will strengthen you. *"May he send you help from the sanctuary, and give you support from Zion"* (v 2). *"Help from the Sanctuary"*—the sanctuary always pictures the place where we meet God. In Israel it was the temple, the place where the Israelite came to get his thoughts straightened and sorted out. There he met with God, heard the word of God, and committed himself to God.

But be reminded that God's sanctuary for us today is the human heart. There God dwells in the Holy of holies of our lives, and we have immediate access through the blood of our Redeemer shed for us. Help from the Sanctuary—where we daily commune with God.

And support from Zion. Zion is another name for Jerusalem, the capital city of the kingdom. In the Scriptures it is also a symbol of the invisible kingdom of God that surrounds us. It is made up of ministering angels sent forth to minister to those who are to be the heirs of salvation. It stands for all the invisible help that God can give you in the day of trouble, in the hour of pressure. While praying, have you ever experienced the "support from Zion?" As Jesus agonized in the garden a ministering angel materialized and strengthened him. He became visible to teach every believer a lesson of what happens when we pray. These ministering angels lift us up when depressed, downcast, discouraged, and defeated. Do not ignore the support you can get from Zion.

The Provision That Sustains You

Our third request for you is found in verse 3, and concerns the marvelous Provision that assures you of the Divine help. *"May he remember all your offerings, and regard with favor your burnt sacrifices"* A moments reflection reveals what our offerings and sacrifices consist of. The author of Hebrews tells us that Our Lord Jesus Christ is the perfect offering and complete sacrifice for all sin for all time. God remembers and regards with favor what Christ has done, and pours out His gracious mercy and love upon us because of that finished work. Paul puts it beautifully in Romans 8:32, *"He that spared not his own Son, but delivered him up for us all, how shall he not with him also freely give us all things?"* There is your guarantee that God is with you, and will grant you all you need.

The Promise That Satisfies You

We offer still another request for you, and it is found in verse 4. *"May he grant you your heart's desire, and fulfill all your plans."* I sincerely hope that more than anything else you want what God wants for you, and that you will be satisfied with nothing less. Surely you want to be confident, courageous, and able to cope with situations, able to handle what comes, and to be trusting and loving. If that is not what you want, it is what God wants for you. And that is our heart's desire for you. Here is God's promise. He will grant you your heart's desire. And he will fulfill your plans. Your plans are the ways you will achieve your heart's desire. It is not that once for all commitment of your life when you said to the Lord that you were making yourself available to Him that is going to see you through. It is the daily decision you make to yield your life anew to the Lord—in times when you feel more nasty than nice—so that His purpose in you can be realized.

Finally, we offer a prayer of praise that anticipates the successful fruition of your desires. *"May we shout for joy over your victory, and in the name of God set up our banners!"* May we shout for joy over your victory. Please understand, then, that victory is never a one-man accomplishment. You do not win your victories by yourself. You might think you do, but you don't. We too have a part in it, and if we are faithful in our prayers, we too can have the joy of sharing in the victorious outcome. You will face difficulties this year. But remember this! Others, who love you, are going to be praying for you and with you in these battles, and encouraging and strengthening you. So when you experience your victories, share them with us that we might share them with you, and rejoice together with you in them. It is sort of like the enthusiastic fans at a football game that joyfully wave their banners as their team marches down the field to gain the victory.

The Response of the King

Now, let me close by suggesting what your response to all of this might be. Verses 6-8 tell us. *"Now I know that the Lord will help his anointed; he will answer him from his holy heaven with mighty victories by his right hand."*

He hasn't even gone out to battle yet, but he is confident of what is going to happen. That's how faith acts. It anticipates victory, and gives thanks in advance for it. That's the kind of response Paul gave when he was in prison. *"Yes, and I shall rejoice. For I know that through your prayers and the help of the Spirit of Jesus Christ this will turn out for my deliverance ... according to my eager expectation and my hope that in nothing I shall be ashamed, but with all boldness as always, so now also Christ shall be magnified in my body whether it be by life or by death." (Phil. 1:19, 20)*

He affirms what is true first of all, and then he stresses what is false. *"Some boast of chariots, and some of horses; but we boast of the name of the Lord our God. They will collapse and fall; but we shall rise and stand upright" (vv. 7, 8).* Horses and chariots are the resources man trusts in, but they are not enough. There are many modern equivalents to those horses and chariots. Here is the note of faith, the quiet, confident expression of a man who has learned where true power lies.

The Benediction. Then the psalm fittingly closes with a benediction that has in it an implied promise of continued prayer. This is a promise to pray for one another. "Give victory to the king, O Lord; answer us when we call."

Father, it is an encouragement to my heart to know that you will grant my desires, and fulfill all my plans. Of course, I want my desires to be focused on what you approve and my plans to conform to your plans for me. Only then can I know the victory you desire to give me.

Things To Ponder

Luther wrote, "Faith alone, which commits itself to God, can sing the song of triumph before the victory and raise the shout of joy before help has been obtained; for to faith all is permitted. It trusts in God, and so really has what it believes, because faith deceives not; as it believes, so is it done."

Psalm 21

"The Glory And Blessing Of the King"

Psalm 21

For the director of music.
A psalm of David.

1 O LORD, **the king rejoices** in your strength.
  How great is his joy in the victories you give!

2 You have granted him the desire of his heart
  and have not withheld the request of his lips. Selah

3 You welcomed him with rich blessings
  and placed a crown of pure gold on his head.

4 He asked you for life, and you gave it to him—
  length of days, forever and ever.

5 Through the victories you gave, his glory is great;
  you have bestowed on him splendor and majesty.

6 Surely you have granted him eternal blessings
  and made him glad with the joy of your presence.

7 For **the king trusts** in the LORD;
  through the unfailing love of the Most High **he will not be shaken.**

8 Your hand will lay hold on all your enemies;
  your right hand will seize your foes.

9 At the time of your appearing you will make them like a fiery furnace.
  In his wrath the LORD will swallow them up, and his fire will consume them.

10 You will destroy their descendants from the earth,
  their posterity from mankind.

11 Though they plot evil against you and devise wicked schemes,
     they cannot succeed;

12 for you will make them turn their backs when you aim
     at them with drawn bow.

13 **Be exalted, O LORD**, in your strength;
     we will sing and praise your might.

NIV

Psalm 21

The King Victorious

If Psalm 20 contains the prayer for the king, Psalm 21 gives the answer to that prayer.

I. The King Rejoices In The Lord. *"O LORD, the king rejoices in your strength."*

    A. For Victories Won. *"How great is his joy in the victories you give!" (v 1)*
    B. For Prayers Answered. *"You have granted him … you have not withheld"*

        1. His asking more than just words—heartfelt. *"the desire of his heart … the request of his lips" (v 2)*
        2. The answer came even before he asked. *"You welcomed (prevented) him with rich blessings and placed a crown of pure gold on his head" (v 3).*
        3. The answer was for far more than he asked. *"He asked you for life, and you gave it to him—length of days, forever and ever" (v 4) 9 See Eph. 3:20)*

    C. For Honor and Dignity Given. *"Though the victories you gave, his glory is great; you have bestowed on him splendor and majesty" (v 5).*

    D. For Eternal Felicity and Intimacy Granted. *"Surely you have granted him eternal blessings and made him glad with the joy of your presence" (v 6).*

II. The King Trusts In The Lord. *"For the king trusts in the LORD; through the unfailing love of the Most High he will not be shaken (moved)" (v 7).*

He remains steadfast because he knows the Lord loves him and will defeat all of his foes.

    A. He seizes them. *"Your hand will lay hold on all your enemies; your right hand will seize your foes" (v 8).*
    B. He consumes them. *"At the time of your appearing you will make them like a fiery furnace. In his wrath the LORD will swallow them up, and his fire will consume them" (v 9).*

C. He cuts off their posterity. *"You will destroy their descendants from the earth their posterity from mankind" (v 10).*
D. He foils their evil plans. *"Though they plot evil against you and devise wicked schemes, they cannot succeed" (v 11)*
E. He puts them in retreat. *"for you will make them turn their backs when you aim at them with drawn bow" (v 12).*

III.The King Exalts The Lord. *"Be exalted, O LORD, in your strength; we will sing and praise your might" (v 13)*

He is able!

A. He Exalts His Name.
B. He Sings His Praises.

Psalm 21

The King Victorious

Psalm 20, as we have seen, is a prayer for the King. It is a prayer that his desire for victory in battle might be successful. That victory, it is recognized, will not be realized by trusting in "chariots and horses" but in the name of the LORD. And the joy of anticipation is seen in the phrase, *"We will shout for joy when you are victorious" (20:5).*

Here in chapter 21, the King returns from battle, and the LORD has blessed him with victory, and the honor that goes along with it. He exclaims, *"How great is his joy in the victories you give!" (v 1).*

The King Rejoices In the LORD

"O Lord, the king rejoices in your strength …" (v 1). There are a number of things he enumerates which constitute the reason for his joy in the Lord. The first one is the most obvious. He is thankful …

For Victories Won.

"How great is his joy in the victories you give!" God had given him strength to subdue his enemies. He is also thankful …

For Prayers Answered.

"You have granted him the desire of his heart and have not withheld the request of his lips. Selah" (v 2). The victory he had so earnestly sought (his heartfelt longing), had been granted by the Lord. It's a good thing when the request of the lips matches the desire of the heart. It means that our whole being is in the asking. God wants to know that our heart and soul is in what we ask.

In fact, the answer had been given even before the victory had been won. *"You welcomed (prevented) him with rich blessings …" (v 3).* The translation "prevent" ordinarily carries the force in English of "hindrance." But here it means "to go before" and has the idea of going before to make the way smooth. So the blessing of victory was assured even before the asking and seeking! *"Before they call, I will answer."*

And furthermore, the answer was for more than the King had asked. *"He asked for life, and you gave it to him (you spared his life),* but also *"length of days, forever and ever" (v 4).*

This doesn't mean that David himself would live forever (although in a sense that is true), but that his reign would be perpetuated forever through those who would succeed him. In Luke, the version of the Christmas story stresses that Joseph was *"a descendant of David."* And the angel's word to Mary was, *"He (the child) will be great and will be called the Son of the Most High. The Lord God will give him the throne of his father David, and he will reign over the house of Jacob forever; his kingdom will never end" (Luke 1:27k, 32, 33).* One will yet sit on David's throne!

He rejoices also ...

For Honor and Dignity Given.

"For the victories you gave, his glory is great; you have bestowed on him splendor and majesty" (v 5). The surrounding nations would hear of his success, and his name would be exalted, and he would be honored and revered. But the King rejoices still further ...

For Eternal Felicity and Intimacy Granted.

"Surely you have granted him eternal blessings and made him glad with the joy of your presence" (v 6). This is certainly the greatest blessing of all. God is pleased with the King and His countenance brightens. He is glad and makes the King glad. It should be a source of great delight for us if something we do makes God happy!

David's rejoicing in the Lord is based on his confidence in the Lord.

The King Trusts In The Lord. *"For the king trusts in the Lord; through the unfailing love (mercy) of the Most High he will not be shaken (moved)."* Mighty warriors are treated like puppets in God's hand as he takes hold of them!

He consumes them.

'At the time of your appearing you will make them like a fiery furnace. In his wrath the LORD will swallow them up, and his fire will consume them" (v 9). David said his trust in the Lord kept him steadfast—unmoved, unshaken. But

this is not so of the wicked. It reminds us of what the author of Hebrews writes, *"At that time (the giving of the Law) his voice shook the earth, but now he has promised, 'One more I will shake not only the earth but also the heavens.' The words "once more" indicate the removing of what can be shaken—that is created things—so that what cannot be shaken may remain. Therefore, since we are receiving a kingdom that cannot be shaken, let us be thankful, and so worship God acceptably with reverence and awe. For our God is a consuming fire"* (Hebrews 12:26-29) How do we convince our unbelieving friends that they are "under the wrath of God" unless they put their trust in the One who bore God's wrath on the cross, a wrath that we deserved? *"Since we have now been justified by his blood, how much more shall we be saved from God's wrath through him!"* ((Romans 5:9). God will one day "swallow" the wicked up in His wrath.

"Your will destroy their descendants from the earth, their posterity from mankind" (v 10).

That is exactly what God did with the Canaanite culture. His judgment on their wickedness was that they should be completely wiped out. Be reminded that once before God looked down on the earth in Noah's day, and He saw that the heart of man was evil **all the time.** As a consequence, the floodwaters wiped man off the face of the earth, save eight souls. I have a good friend who doesn't like to talk about the wrath of God. He feels we ought to major on God's love, and I fully agree, but I reminded him that like a jeweler displaying his diamonds against a black backdrop, God displays His grace against the blackness of sin's night. Peter reminded his detractors that God *"is not slow in keeping is promise, as some understand slowness. He is patient with you, not wanting anyone to perish, but everyone to come to repentance.* And then he writes in effect, "But God's wrath is coming. It's just ahead when everything will be consumed by fire at the coming of the Lord." And if unbelievers are not ready, it will be too late to get ready then.

But I have digressed from our study. The psalmist goes on to say ...

He foils their evil plans.

"Though they plot evil against you and devise wicked schemes, they cannot succeed." He puts them in full retreat. *"... for you will make them turn their backs when you aim at them with drawn bow" (v 12).* Of course, God is the Most High, Sovereign of the Universe, and He will give to the wicked exactly what they so justly deserve.

The King Exalts The Lord.

"Be exalted, O LORD, in your strength; we will sing and praise your might" (v 13). God is so able. His power and might are unimaginable. David ends this psalm as he begins Psalm 34

   "Glorify the Lord with me; let us exalt his name together."

Father, I thank you that though once your enemy, I am now a friend, reconciled through our Lord Jesus. I would not want to be counted among your enemies when the day of wrath comes. I'm grateful, too, for the victories which are ours through Christ's smashing victory at the cross "having disarmed the powers and authorities, he made a public spectacle of them triumphing over them by the cross." Therefore, we can "stand against the devil's schemes," and echo David's gratitude for victories won.

Things To Ponder

David reminds us that the highest use of a shaken time is to discover the unshakeable. When everything around is tottering, then is the time to get our eyes on what stands firm. When the author of Hebrews speaks about the Lord he is "Jesus Christ, the same, yesterday, today and forever." So when "change and decay in all around I see," we can say, "O Thou that changes not, abide with me."

Psalm 22

"My God, My God Why?"

Psalm 22

For the director of music.
To [the tune of] "The Doe of the Morning."

A psalm of David.

1 My God, my God, why have you forsaken me?
        Why are you so far from saving me,
        so far from the words of my groaning?
2 O my God, I cry out by day, but you do not answer,
        by night, and am not silent.

3 Yet you are enthroned as the Holy One;
        you are the praise of Israel.
4 In you our fathers put their trust;
        they trusted and you delivered them.
5 They cried to you and were saved;
        in you they trusted and were not disappointed.

6 But I am a worm and not a man,
        scorned by men and despised by the people.

7 All who see me mock me;
        they hurl insults, shaking their heads:
8 "He trusts in the LORD; let the LORD rescue him.
        Let him deliver him, since he delights in him."

9 Yet you brought me out of the womb;
        you made me trust in you even at my mother's breast.
10 From birth I was cast upon you;
        from my mother's womb you have been my God.
11 Do not be far from me, for trouble is near
        and there is no one to help.

12 Many bulls surround me;
        strong bulls of Bashan encircle me.

13 Roaring lions tearing their prey
>   open their mouths wide against me.
14 I am poured out like water,
>   and all my bones are out of joint.
>   My heart has turned to wax;
>   it has melted away within me.
15 My strength is dried up like a potsherd,
>   and my tongue sticks to the roof of my mouth;
>   you lay me in the dust of death.
16 Dogs have surrounded me;
>   a band of evil men has encircled me,
>   they have pierced my hands and my feet.
17 I can count all my bones;
>   people stare and gloat over me.
18 They divide my garments among them
>   and cast lots for my clothing.
19 But you, O LORD, be not far off;
>   O my Strength, come quickly to help me.
20 Deliver my life from the sword,
>   my precious life from the power of the dogs.
21 Rescue me from the mouth of the lions;
>   save me from the horns of the wild oxen.

22 I will declare your name to my brothers;
>   in the congregation I will praise you.
23 You who fear the LORD, praise him!
>   All you descendants of Jacob, honor him!
>   Revere him, all you descendants of Israel!
24 For he has not despised or disdained the suffering of the afflicted one;
>   he has not hidden his face from him
>   but has listened to his cry for help.

25 From you comes the theme of my praise in the great assembly;
>   before those who fear you will I fulfill my vows.
26 The poor will eat and be satisfied;
>   they who seek the LORD will praise him—may your hearts
>   live forever!
27 All the ends of the earth will remember and turn to the LORD,
>   and all the families of the nations will bow down before him,

28 for dominion belongs to the LORD
    and he rules over the nations.

29 All the rich of the earth will feast and worship;
        all who go down to the dust will kneel before him—
        those who cannot keep themselves alive.
30 Posterity will serve him;
        future generations will be told about the Lord.
31 They will proclaim his righteousness to a people yet unborn—
        for he has done it.

NIV

Psalm 22

The Agony and The Ecstasy

The psalm divides into two parts: the first part, a graphic description of sorrow and suffering as the Victim writhes in agony nailed to a tree; the second part a hymn of praise, as the same Victim—now Victor—in ecstasy contemplates the gathering of the Gentiles, even the high and mighty, to pay him homage in worship, and the triumphant good news going out to generations yet unborn.

I. The Crucifixion. (Humiliation)

A. The cry of dereliction. "*My God, my God, why have you forsaken me?* "*Why are you far from saving me, so far from the words of my groaning? O my God, I cry out by day, but you do not answer, by night, and am not silent*"(*v 1, 2*).

B. A statement of dismay. "*our fathers … trusted and you delivered them. They cried to you and were saved; in you they trusted and were not disappointed*" (*v 3-5*) The inference seems to be, "Why are you treating me differently? I have trusted you, but am not delivered. I cry to you, but no answer comes."

C. An expression of utter rejection. "*But I am a worm and not a man, scorned by men and despised by the people. All who see me mock me; they hurl insults, shaking their heads: "He trusts in the LORD; let the LORD rescue him. let him deliver him, since he delights in him*" (*v 6-8*).

    1. Scorned.

    2. Despised.

    3. Mocked.

    4. Insulted.

    5. Maligned

D. An affirmation of his trust in God, and a cry for help. "*Yet **you** brought me out of the womb; **you** made me trust in you even at my mother's breast. From birth I was cast upon **you**; from my mother's womb **you** have been my God. Do not be far from me, for trouble is near and there is no one to help*" (*v 9-11*).

E. A graphic description of his agony on the cross.

    1. The bestial crowd. "*Many bulls surround me; strong bulls of Bashan encircle me. Roaring lions tearing their prey open their mouths wide against me*" (*v 12, 13*).

2. The ebbing strength. *"I am poured out like water …" (v 14).*

3. The dislocated joints. *"… and all my bones are out of joint" (v 14).*

4. The heart trauma (that may have issued in a ruptured heart). *"My heart has turned to wax; it has melted away within me" (v 14).*

5. The dehydration. *"My strength is dried up like a potsherd, and my tongue sticks to the roof of my mouth; you lay me in the dust of death" (v 15).*

6. The cruel piercing of the flesh. *"Dogs have surrounded me; a band of evil men has encircled me, they have pierced my hands and my feet" (v 16).*

7. The humiliation and shame. *"I can count all my bones; people stare and gloat over me" (v 17).*

8. The gambling for garments. *"They divide my garments among them and cast lots for my clothing" (v 18).*

F. Come to my help! My life, my dearest possession, is all I have left. (In Luke 23:46, Jesus prays to the Father, *"Father into your hands I commit my spirit."* This is actually a quote from Psalm 31:5.)" *But you, O LORD, be not far off; O my Strength, come quickly to help me. Deliver my life from the sword, my precious life (my afflicted soul) from the power of the dogs. Rescue me from the mouth of the lions; save me from the horns of the wild oxen" (v 19-21).* (In the RV there is a dramatic and sudden change. There is a moment of silence signaling perhaps Christ's death, followed by the feast of deliverance and celebration signaling God's power in resurrection.)

II. The Resurrection. (Exaltation)

A. The note of celebration. *"I will declare your name to my brothers; in the congregation I will praise you" (v 22).*

B. The call goes out for Israel to join in the celebration. *"You who fear the LORD, praise him! All you descendants of Jacob, honor him! Revere him, all you descendants of Israel! For he has not despised or disdained the suffering of the afflicted one; he has not hidden his face from him but has listened to his cry for help" (v 23-24).*

C. Every knee shall bow and every tongue confess! *"From you comes the theme of my praise in the great assembly; before those who fear you will I fulfill my vows. The poor will eat and be satisfied; they who seek the LORD will praise him—may your hearts live forever! All the ends of the earth will remember and turn to the LORD, and all the families of the nations will bow down before him, for dominion belongs to the LORD and he rules over the nations. All the rich of the earth will feast and worship; all who go down to the dust will kneel before him—those who cannot keep themselves alive. Posterity will serve him; future generations will be told about the Lord they will proclaim his righteousness to a people yet unborn ..."(v 25-31).*

1. The poor and humble; the rich and proud.
2. All the ends of the earth; all the families of the nations
3. All future generations, yet unborn.

He has done it! He has done it! "It is finished!" *(v 31).*

The Agony and The Ecstasy

Psalm 22

This psalm has become so perfectly and properly associated with our Lord Jesus Christ, that it is almost impossible to read it in any other way. Surely the description here could not apply to any experience through which David went even though he was often in peril. This and the two chapters that follow constitute a triad of truths regarding our Lord in His work as Savior, Shepherd, and Sovereign.

Jesus quoted the first words and the last words of this psalm as he hung on the cross. Therefore, we are justified in reading it in the light of the cross. It has two great movements. The first part is a graphic description of sorrow and suffering as the Victim writhes in agony nailed to a tree, and the second part is a hymn of praise as the same Victim—now a Victor—in ecstasy contemplates the gathering of Jew and Gentiles to worship and celebrate what God has done. The rich and the poor, the high and the low pay him homage, and the nations bow to his sovereignty. The news goes out even to generations yet unborn.

It is an amazing psalm for it pictures both the crucifixion and resurrection of our Lord Jesus Christ, painted by David the psalmist one thousand years before Christ was born into our world. It constitutes one of the most astonishing predictions of all time. The reader is reminded that crucifixion as a mode of execution wasn't even invented until roughly 600 BC. It was probably first introduced by the Phoenicians and Carthaginians at that time, from whom the Romans got it. The Jewish mode of execution was stoning. No Jew was put to death by crucifixion until sometime late in the inter-testamental period. Yet here, hundreds of years earlier, David describes it in graphic terms. Crucifixion is described in minute detail, far more detail that the Gospels afford us. The chance that all this could have occurred by accident is beyond the realm of probability and possibility. Yet all was fulfilled as predicted in this psalm.

Ray Stedman in his book *Folk Psalms of Faith* alludes to the assassination of President John Kennedy in Dallas on November 22, 1963. Suppose, he writes, there had been in existence a document which predicted this event and which we knew to have been written in A.D. 963. That was about the time of the height of the Byzantine Empire, when most of the Western world was ruled from Constantinople, barbarian tribes only sparsely inhabited much of Europe, and America was not yet discovered. Suppose this document predicted that a man of great prominence, head of a great nation, would be riding down a street of a large city in a metal chariot not drawn by horses, and would suddenly and violently die from the penetration of his brain by a little piece of metal hurled from a weapon made of wood and iron, aimed at him from the window of a tall building, and that his death would have worldwide effect and cause global mourning. You can imagine the awe such a document would hold today. (*Folk Psalms of Faith*, p 66)

The Crucifixion. (Humiliation)

1. A Cry of Dereliction. *"My God, my God, why have you forsaken me?"*

These opening words have been called "the cry of dereliction," that is, the cry of abandonment as the sufferer becomes aware that he is forsaken by His God. As we know from the New Testament, Jesus uttered these words at the end of a strange period of darkness that settled upon the land.

The deep question here is whether Jesus had only, on account of bodily weakness and a temporary obscuration of the inward vision, a sense of being abandoned, or whether, in any real sense, God had actually forsaken Him. Luther and Calvin allowed themselves to say that in the hours which preceded this cry our Lord endured the torments of the damned. And Rambach, whose *Meditations on the Sufferings of Christ* have fueled the piety of Germany for a hundred years, says:

> "God was now dealing with Him not as a loving and merciful father with His child, but as an offended and righteous judge with an evildoer. The heavenly Father now regards His Son as the greatest sinner to be found beneath the sun, and discharges on Him the whole weight of His wrath."

Even when saying that, we find ourselves only in the shallows near the shore; the unplumbed mysterious ocean lies beyond. How can we begin to understand that statement in Isaiah 53, *"Yet we did esteem him stricken, smitten of God, and afflicted?"* (*v 4*). Or again in the same chapter, *"Yet it pleased the Lord to bruise Him; He has put Him to grief ..."* (*v 10*). Or moving quickly to the New Testament, think of Paul's words in 2 Corinthians 5:21, *"He (God) made Him (Jesus) who knew no sin to be sin for us, that we might become the righteousness of God in Him."* He became what we are, in order to make us what He is! Glorious fact! And Paul, in writing to the Galatians said, *"Christ has redeemed us from the curse of the law, having become a curse for us—for it is written, "Cursed is everyone who hangs on a tree" (Galatians 3:13).*

Personally, I can only respond as the apostle responded in awe and wonder to say simply, *"He loved me, and gave himself for me." Can I explain it? No. Do I believe it? O yes!*

> *Were the whole ream of nature mine,*
> *That were a present far too small:*
> *Love so amazing, so divine,*
> *Demands my soul, my life, my all. (Isaac Watts)*

2. A statement of dismay.

The Agony of Crucifixion. "But I am a worm, and no man."

For some strange reason God is treating him differently. Even the spectators reflect that difference. He is treated like a despised and hated criminal, as though he had lost his right to live in human society. Matthew records for us the fact that the crowd actually used these very words. The unthinking multitude passing by, looking at the sufferer on the cross, cried, "He trusts in God; let God deliver him now." What an amazing prediction that is! The very words that could not have been controlled, and who had no intention of fulfilling prophecy, are clearly foretold.

This one as He speaks declares that there are no grounds for abandonment in himself. *"God made him to be sin for us, He who knew no sin; that we might be made the righteousness of God in him."*

The self-image people find this reference repulsive—imagine speaking of yourself as a worm! Even the hymnists have changed Isaac Watts original verse from "such a worm as I" to "for sinners such as I!"

> Alas! and did my Savior bleed?
> And did my Sov'reign die?
> Would He devote that sacred head
> For sinners such as I! (For such a worm as I)

Someone has suggested that Jesus became what we are in order to make us what He is. The self-image concept that man must have is just this—prior to salvation. After that, our self-image radically changes, because we are now God's children, and of great worth and value to God. As someone has said,

God does not love us because we are valuable; we are valuable because God loves us!

The sufferer goes on to describe the scene from the cross. He uses poetic figures to describe the onlookers—bulls (wild oxen) and lions.

Then he describes His own reaction. What a description of sheer exhaustion, weariness, pain, and fatigue. This was set down when no one, so far as history records, put anyone to death by crucifixion. Certainly, the Jews did not, for their method of execution was to stone someone to death. Stripped shamefully, He can see and feel his bones all pulled out of joint. His feet and hands were pierced. Even to the detail of lots being cast for His seamless tunic.

He offers a final prayer (19-21) that is equivalent to Christ's words on the cross, *"Father, into your hands I commit my spirit."* (Actually a quotation from Psalm 31:5). If anyone is going to lift me out of the dust of death, raise me up again, it will be you. I trust myself to You, Father!

The Triumph of Resurrection. *"I will declare your name to my brothers . . ." (v 22).*

There seems to be a broken and unfinished strophe at the end of verse 21. That suddenly interrupted strophe suggests the hushing of the voice of Jesus in death. The speech suddenly resumes, but in tones of triumph. There is a period of silence in the sequence of the narrative. Then without a word of explanation the same speaker goes on. Here, unquestionably, is the Resurrection. The same one who has just suffered and died is now in the midst of a company whom he calls his brethren. The writer of Hebrews picks up on this theme: He applies these words to Jesus, an says that it was the will and purpose of God the Father to bring many sons to glory, and that it was fitting that he should make the captain of their salvation perfect through suffering. And, he continues, *"So Jesus is not ashamed to call them brothers. He says, 'I will declare your name to my brothers; in the presence of the congregation I will sing your praises"* (Hebrews 2:11, 12). This is a quote from this psalm.

> *Father, Thank you that we have been brought into your family through the suffering of our Lord Jesus. I am one of the "many sons" you are bringing to glory! Paul reminds me in Romans that I am an "heir and a joint-heir" with Christ. What a privilege!*

Things To Ponder

Was the "cup" from which Jesus asked to be delivered, death? We know He came to die for us, but the cup probably represents the aloneness He felt to be soon abandoned and forsaken by the Father as He bore the whole weight of man's sins on himself. He was without sin, but now He was to be "made sin for us." The reality of that was so painful for Him that Jesus' sweat became like great drops of blood" (Luke 22:44). We are aware of His awful sufferings, but we must never forget His agonizing cry "My God, My God why have your forsaken Me?"

Psalm 23

"The Lamb's Shepherd"

Psalm 23

A psalm of David.

1 The LORD is my shepherd,
   I shall not be in want.

2 He makes me lie down in green pastures,
   he leads me beside quiet waters,

3 he restores my soul.
   He guides me in paths of righteousness for his name's sake.

4 Even though I walk through the valley of the shadow of death,
   I will fear no evil, for you are with me;
   your rod and your staff, they comfort me.

5 You prepare a table before me in the presence of my enemies.
   You anoint my head with oil; my cup overflows.

6 Surely goodness and love will follow me all the days of my life,
   and I will dwell in the house of the LORD forever.

NIV

The Lamb's Shepherd

Psalm 23

David assumes the role of a lamb in the flock, makes a declaration, and draws a deduction from it in verse 1.

"The Lord is my Shepherd"
"I Shall Lack Nothing"

I. The Shepherd Goes Before Me To Lead Me And Guide Me.

A. **Rest & Refreshment.** "He makes me lie down in green pastures" "He leads me beside still waters."
B. **Restoration & Redirection.** *"He restores My Soul"* *"He guides me in paths of righteousness for His name's sake"*

II. The Shepherd Walks Beside Me To Encourage And Comfort Me.

A. **Courage.** *"I will fear no evil for you are with me"*
B. **Comfort.** *"Your rod and your staff, they comfort me"*

III. The Shepherd Moves Around Me To Provide For Me And To Protect Me.

A. **Provision.** *"You prepare a table before me"*
B. **Protection.** *"in the presence of my enemies"*

IV. The Shepherd Ministers To Me To Heal and To Help Me.

A. **Healing** *"You anoint my head with oil"*
B. **Helping** *"My cup overflows"*

V. The Shepherd Follows After Me To Lead Me Home.

A. **Heading Home.** *"Goodness and mercy will follow (pursue) me all the days of my life"*
B. **Safely Home** *"and I will dwell in the house of the Lord forever."*

God has given us the power of *imaging. Imagination* means mentally visualizing. A long held visualization could become determinative. So memorize this little psalm if you haven't already, and use it to bring inward peace and calm in the midst of trying times.

Psalm 23

The Lamb's Shepherd

As we begin our brief study of this very familiar psalm, it might be good for us to remind ourselves that the whole history of God's people, Israel, is bound up with shepherds and sheep. All Israel's great leaders were shepherds—Abel, Abraham, Isaac, Jacob, Joseph, Moses, and David. The striking image of the Shepherd and the sheep is one used frequently in the Scriptures. I love Isaiah's description of Yahweh, the Sovereign Lord,

> *"He tends his flock like a shepherd: He gathers the lambs in his arms and carries them close to his heart; he gently leads those that have young" (Isaiah 40:11).*

This psalm has sung its way across the barriers of time, race, and language. For over twenty-five centuries it has been treasured in the hearts of people. Today it is more beloved than ever before. Why is this so? Because it assures us that Our Great Shepherd knows his sheep one by one, is abundantly able to provide, guide and protect them, and at the close of the day open the door to the sheepfold—that house not made with hands. It reminds us that the Lord is the Supply for all our wants, the Strength for all our weakness, and the Surety for all our way.

Alexander Maclaren believed that the psalm was written by David in his later years, and David is reflecting back on how the Lord had guided and directed him all those intervening years since had had tended his father's flocks on the hillsides outside of Bethlehem. He also suggests, as many expositor's do, that the psalm fall into two halves: the first half setting the Lord forth as a Shepherd, and us as the sheep of his pasture; the second gives Him as the Host, and us as the guests at His table and the dwellers in His house.

That may well be, but it seems to me that the Lord is the Shepherd through-out, and the narrative begins with the sheep being led from the fold by the Shepherd, and describes His directing and protecting them through a day's journey. Maybe we could call this psalm 'A Day in the Life of a Lamb."

The Shepherd leads the flock out, and when they have traveled a ways and are tired, he makes them rest "in green pastures" and find refreshment "beside still waters." Then as they move onward, prone to wander as sheep are (Isaiah

53:6) they get off the path, and "He restores" them and redirects them to the "right" paths. They pass through a deep, dark ravine where the Shepherd comes along side to encourage and comfort they. He brings they out on to a "tableland" where they graze contentedly while the Shepherd walks the perimeter of the pasture to make sure they are safe from predators. Wounds are inflicted along the way by briers and thorns, and the Shepherd pauses to tenderly care for their wounds by anointing them with oil. They are soothed and satisfied. And finally, as the day begins to fade, the Shepherd takes up the rear and herds them back to the safety of the sheepfold assisted, perhaps by two sheepdogs, "Goodness and Mercy." The psalmist extrapolates "day" to "all the days of my life" and ends in the place of ultimate safety and contentment "the house of the Lord."

David here assumes the role of a lamb in the flock, makes a declaration, and draws a deduction from it in verse 1, "The Lord is my Shepherd, I shall not want." The Old Prayer Book rendering is "therefore I can lack nothing." It is true that because He is our Shepherd, we will not want, but more than that, we would greatly lack but for the Shepherd; that in ourselves we do lack, but that this lack is made good by the sufficiency of the Shepherd. He is my great Complement! What I have not, He has. What I am not, He is. No matter how much I lack, and my lack is enormous, all that I lack, He is, and so I am always complete in Him. Isn't that what Paul says in Colossians 2 when he writes, we are *"complete or full in Him?"* For every point where I am empty, there is Christ with His sufficiency to fill up that lack with Himself. He is the great I AM, Yahweh, the Covenant keeping God who gives Himself away to His people, saying, "All you lack I will be to you. And the apostle John pictures our Lord Jesus as the Great I AM who is to His own all they need for this life and the next.

I AM the water of life
I AM the bread of life
I AM the light of life
I AM the door to life
I AM the good Shepherd who gives life to the full
I AM the resurrection and the life
I AM the way, the truth and the life
I AM the vine life.

Yes, Jesus is our Great and Good Shepherd who gives His life for the sheep, who came to give life and give it to the full, who knows His sheep and is known by them, who keeps them in safe in the hollow of His hand!

With those wonderful reminders, let us reflect for a few moments how the Lord, our Shepherd, meets every lack in our lives.

The Shepherd Goes Before Me To Lead Me and Guide Me.

He searches out a place where the sheep's need for rest and refreshment can occur. **Rest.** *"He makes me lie down in green pastures"* The shepherd starts the sheep grazing about 4 o'clock in the morning. They walk steadily as they graze, and are rarely still. By 12:00 o'clock, the sun is beating down and the sheep are hot, tired, and thirsty. The wise shepherd knows that sheep must not drink when it is hot, and their stomach is filled with undigested grass. So he make them lie down in green pastures, a cool, soft place. The sheep will not eat lying down, so they chew the cud, which is nature's way of digestion.

It is easier for us to work for the Lord than to rest in the Lord. Sometimes the Lord has to actually and literally put us on our backs to give us a chance to look up, so to speak. He "makes me" lie down! He imposes His will on us so that we have to get quiet. I love Whittier's verse,

Drop Thy still dews of quietness,
Till all our striving cease;
Take from our souls the strain and stress,
And let our ordered lives confess
The beauty of Thy peace.

Refreshment. The second phrase speaks to us of refreshment. "He leads me beside the still waters (waters of rest or quietness)." Sheep are timid creatures. They are instinctively afraid of swiftly moving water, and for good reason. Their heavy coat makes it difficult to swim. So they will not drink from a swift current for fear of falling in. Sometimes the shepherd fashions a dam across a small stream to form a pool that is still.

Reflections on these images can reduce the tension in our lives. Our Shepherd wants us to rest in Him, and to be refreshed by Him.

Restoration. Rest and refreshment restore the sheep. So this may refer to what has gone before. But all sheep seem to have the dubious distinction of wandering, of going astray. Isaiah 53:6 speaks of that tendency, *"We all, like sheep, have gone astray, each of us have turned to his own way ..."* Sheep have this peculiar aptitude of leaving the shepherd, as well as for following him. So, in this sense they need to be restored. The Shepherd counts his sheep, and when one is missing, he leaves the others in the fold and goes out in search of the one that is lost, and when he finds it, brings it back on his shoulders rejoicing. If it occurs repeatedly, he sometimes breaks the leg of the sheep, then carries it close until it heals.

O to grace how great a debtor
Daily I'm constrained to be!
Let Thy goodness, like a fetter,
Bind my wandering heart to Thee:
Prone to wander, Lord, I feel it,
Prone to leave the God I love;
Here's my heart, O take and seal it;
Seal it for Thy courts above.

Isaiah calls this tendency to wander "iniquity." But God laid on His Son the *"iniquity of us all."*

Redirection. *"He guides me in paths of righteousness for His name's sake."*

This suggests that the Shepherd imposes His will on the sheep to bring them back to the path of rectitude from which they have strayed. Sheep have very little sense of direction. They have poor eyesight, and cannot see very far ahead. Sometimes the shepherd leads them over steep and difficult places, and they must stay close to him and trust his judgment. Are we willing to trust that He knows the way that is best for us, although that way may seem dark and difficult? In fact, that is the very next place the shepherd leads the flock. He guides *"for His name's sake"* which probably means "for the sake of His reputation." In a sense, a shepherd is evaluated by how well his flock is cared for, just as a parent is evaluated on how well a child turns out.

Against a backdrop of false shepherds abusing the people, Ezekiel speaks of God returning to His oppressed people as their shepherd to give them rest,

> *"For this what the Sovereign Lord says: I myself will search for my sheep and look after them. As a shepherd looks after his scattered flock when he is with them, so will I look after my sheep. I will rescue them from all the places where they were scattered on a day of clouds and darkness. I will bring them out from the nations and gather them from the countries and I will bring them into their own land. There they will\ lie down in good grazing land, and there they will feed in a rich pasture on*

the mountains of Israel. I Myself will tend my sheep and have them lie down (lead them to rest), declares the Sovereign Lord. I will search for the lost and bring back the strays. I will bind up the injured and strengthen the weak, but the sleek and the strong I will destroy. I will shepherd the flock with justice."

Did Ezekiel have David's psalm in mind?

The Shepherd Walks Beside Me To Encourage Me And To Comfort Me. *"Even though I walk through the valley of the shadow of death."*

Courage. Henry Ward Beecher called the 23rd Psalm the nightingale of the Psalms, because the nightingale sings its sweetest song in the darkest night. Death is the dark night of the soul. We fear death because it is an unknown and untraveled way. Actually, this could be any "glen of gloom." It is a shadowed way. Deep dark ravines slit the hill country of Palestine. Dangers lurk there. Now the Shepherd comes and walks with his sheep, stays close by them, to instill in them courage. *"I will fear no evil, for you are with me."* Someone has observed that God goes before us when the way is smooth, but He stands beside us when the way is dangerous and dark. And He possesses the weapons to ward off any hidden danger. That is comforting.

Comfort. *Your rod and staff, they comfort me."* The rod and staff were for protection and assistance. The rod was a short club-like instrument used as a weapon to fight off predators. The staff was longer, sometimes with a crook on the end, to keep the sheep from wandering too far. The promise still stands, *"I will never desert you, nor will I ever forsake you" (Heb. 13:5).*

The Shepherd Moves Around Me To Provide for Me and To Protect Me. **"***You prepare a table before me in the presence of my enemies."*

The shepherd leads the sheep out of the dark ravine an on to a "tableland." He prepares the pasturage by removing anything harmful to the flock, and then allows them to graze. He patrols the perimeter to make sure they are safe "in the presence of enemies." Thus, the shepherd continues to provide for them and protectively watch over them. Here also there is leisure time to attend to the sheep individually, providing the healing oil and the overflowing cup.

The Shepherd Ministers To Me To Heal and To Help Me.

Healing. "You anoint my head with oil." The shepherd provides for the sheep in the same way a gracious host would provide for the weary traveler. Hospitality in a Bedouin household included food, lodging, and even protection. The head was anointed as a token of honor, but here it probably refers to a soothing balm for hurts incurred along the way from brier and thorn.

Helping. "My cup overflows." It is as if the sheep is saying, "It can't get any better than this!" The overflowing cup speaks of generosity. It was not half-full, but running over. Every need is abundantly met. The sheep feel the security, significance, and satisfaction offered by their shepherd.

The Shepherd Follows After Me To Direct Me Back To The Sheepfold.

Heading Home. *"Goodness and mercy will follow me (pursue me) all the days of my life."* Perhaps as light begins to wane, the shepherd retraces his steps, and herds the sheep back to the fold. Perhaps it is a stretch, but someone has suggested that "Goodness and Mercy" might refer to two sheep dogs nipping at the flock to hurry them along.

Safely Home. *"And I will dwell in the house of the Lord forever."* The phrases *"all the days of my life"* and *"dwell in the house of the Lord forever"* move this simple "day in the life of a lamb" well beyond the immediate. This is the way the Good Shepherd has treated David all through his life. He will not only help him find his way home, but assure him of an eternal home. The temple had not been built yet in David's day, but he often speaks of the "house of the Lord' referring to the wilderness tabernacle and the Holy of Holies (See Psalm 26-28). There he could meet with God, behold His glory, and feel secure in His care. Could Jesus have had David's concluding word in mind when He sought to comfort His fearful disciples in John 14, *"In my Father's house are many mansions (abiding places). If it were not so I would have told you. I go and prepare a place for you …?"*

Only those who know the Shepherd, and are one of His can know this with confidence. *"My sheep hear my voice, and I know them, and they follow me; and I give eternal life to them, and they shall never perish; and no one shall snatch them out of My hand"* (John 10:27-28).

Lord, you are not a stranger to me, for you tell me, "I know my sheep and my sheep know me. You call me by name! Nor are you like a thief who comes only to steal and kill and destroy. You did not come to take, but to give-life to the full. Nor are you like a hired hand that cuts and runs when the wolf approaches. You protect me, and see me through the dark places in life. Thank you, Good Shepherd!

Things To Ponder

God has given us the power of *imaging*. *Imagination* means mentally visualizing. A long held visualization could become determinative. So memorize this little psalm if you haven't already, and use it to bring inward peace and calm in the midst of trying times.

Psalm 24

"The King of Glory"

Psalm 24

Of David. A psalm.

1 The earth is the Lord's, and everything in it,
    the world, and all who live in it;
2 for he founded it upon the seas
    and established it upon the waters.

3 Who may ascend the hill of the LORD?
    Who may stand in his holy place?

4 He who has clean hands and a pure heart,
    who does not lift up his soul to an idol or swear by what is false.

5 He will receive blessing from the LORD
    and vindication from God his Savior.

6 Such is the generation of those who seek him,
    who seek your face, O God of Jacob. Selah

7 Lift up your heads, O you gates;
    be lifted up, you ancient doors,
    that the King of glory may come in.

8 Who is this King of glory?
    The LORD strong and mighty,
    the LORD mighty in battle.

9 Lift up your heads, O you gates;
    lift them up, you ancient doors,
    that the King of glory may come in.

10 Who is he, this King of glory?
    The LORD Almighty—he is the King of glory. Selah.

NIV

Psalm 24

King Of My Life

I. King of The Universe. We are not our own, but His.

A. The reach of His sovereignty. *"The earth is the Lord's, and everything in it, the world, and all who live in it" (v 1).*
B. The reason for His sovereignty. *"He founded it … established it" (v 1)*

II. King Of My Life. Give Him your undivided love and loyalty.

A. The One Who May Ascend and Stand In His Presence

1. Clean hands
2. Pure heart
3. Fiercely loyal
4. A Seeking heart

B. Such a one is

1. Blessed
2. Vindicated

III. King Of Glory.

Open the temple gates of your life and let Him rule supreme.

A. He Waits For Us To Open To Him *"Lift up your heads, O you gates; be lifted up, you ancient doors, that the King of glory may come in" (v 7, 9).*
B. One Day Every Knee Shall Bow and Every Tongue Confess. *"The LORD strong and mighty, the LORD mighty in battle … The LORD Almighty—he is the King of glory" (v 9, 10).*

Psalm 24

King Of My Life—
I Crown Thee Now

I have always loved this psalm for its poetic majesty, and I hear its great themes set to music resounding in my heart and mind. But I confess to you that I have not spent that much time thinking about it, meditating on it, and asking what the Lord wants to say to my heart personally. That is, not until recently, when I have brought it to mind repeatedly, even thinking about it when I awakened in the middle of the night So I determined to put something together. The Lord helped me in my understanding, and blessed my heart, and I want to share some of these thoughts with you.

The occasion of this psalm seems to be the bringing up of the Ark of the Covenant by David to Jerusalem, after he became king. The Philistines had captured the ark during the closing days of Eli the priest. Eli's sons died, and the ark was captured. The Philistines did not fare well with the ark in their possession. Wherever they put it disaster followed. Finally they sent it back to Israel to Beth Shemesh. Some of the men of that village, overcome with curiosity, dared to look inside the ark, and God struck seventy of them dead. The people of the village were terrified, and cried out "Who can stand in the presence of the Lord, this holy God?" (I Samuel 6:20) The ark was moved to the home of Abinadab in Kiriath-jearim, and lay neglected for 20 years.

Saul's reign began and ended. David was anointed and eventually became king, and his reign flourished. He completed the conquest of the Philistines, and captured the city of Jebus, which he renamed Jerusalem. Finally, David decided it was time to bring the Ark of the Covenant back into the camp of Israel. He located the ark, put it on a cart like a piece of furniture, and led the people in praiseful procession toward Jerusalem. The cart hit a rut in the road, and began to sway, and Uzzah, a godly man, reached out to steady the ark, and like one who encounters a high-tension wire, he was struck dead.

David was angry, fearful and frustrated, and cried out, "How can the ark of the Lord ever come to me?" He left the ark in the care of Obed-Edom the Gittite, where it stayed for three months.

David tries again. This time he followed carefully the instructions given to Moses by God many years before. The ark was to be carried on poles inserted into loops on its sides. Again there was great excitement, choirs singing, musicians playing, and dancers dancing. David offered sacrifices to the Lord. He danced mightily before the Lord, and finally the joyful procession arrived at the city gates, and, with one voice, they cried out for the gatekeepers to open to them.

The story of the ark is the story of approaching the presence of the LORD. In captive hands, it led to devastation and judgment. In curious hands, in meant instant retribution. Even in conscientious hands, it meant death. The ark was a symbol of God's holy presence in the midst of his people. It was the throne of God on earth, modeled after the heavenly throne with the overshadowing cherubim. How does one approach such an awesome, holy God? Obviously, the Ark of the Covenant was removed from its original setting within the Holy of Holies in the Wilderness Tabernacle. Symbolically, the only way to come into the presence of a holy God was by means of the appointed sacrifice whose blood was carried by the High Priest there before the Mercy Seat or Throne of God once a year to atone for the sins of the people.

David was certainly aware of this, but salvation is not in view here in the psalm. David is seeking to answer the question, How can we live in His presence? What kind of life pleases God? What does God require of His creation, and more particularly His "new" creation?

The answer is important for us, and we dare not ignore its implications for our lives.

Know first, David says, that this LORD that we serve is …

King of The Universe. *"The earth is the LORD'S, and everything in it, the world, and all who live in it" (v 1).*

Do not pass over this sentence lightly as you may have done many times before. It reveals a most basic, fundamental truth for the life of every person. It gives us first of all **the reach of God's sovereignty.**

> The earth is the LORD'S.
> Everything in the earth is the LORD'S.
> All who live on the earth are the LORD'S.

And **the reason for His sovereignty** is given in verse 2. *"He founded it … He established it.* "The earth is the Lord's, and everything in it, and those who dwell in it," because He created them. What God originates is His own, and belongs to Him for his own purpose. Just as an inventor has exclusive ownership over his invention; a designer has exclusive ownership over his design; a builder has exclusive ownership over his building; the Creator has exclusive ownership over his creation.

When the apostle John is granted a vision of the heavenly throne room in the 4th chapter of Revelation, he sees God on the throne of the universe in gemstone brilliance, and he hears the heavenly worship team praising God, casting their crowns before the throne and singing, *"You are worthy, our Lord and God, to receive glory and honor and power, for **you created all things, and by your will they were created and have their being.**" (4:11).*

The Scriptures highlight three basic principles that if understood and obeyed would deliver every life from conflict and unrest.

> Everything exists for God.
> Everything belongs to God.
> Everything comes from God.

If we understood and obeyed the first of these, that "everything exists for God," our lives would be delivered from Egotism, the prideful attitude that puts us at the center instead of God.

If we understood and obeyed the second principle, that "everything belongs to God," it would deliver us from Materialism, the incessant quest for more possessions or things. We would recognize that we are not owners, but trustees, put here to manage Another's goods rather than our own.

And finally, if we understood and obeyed the third principle, that "everything comes from God, it would deliver us from Sensualism, the desire for illegitimate pleasures that war against the soul.

We can approach God through the atoning work of Christ, but once we are in His presence, how do we live before Him? We cannot live in the presence of God unless we recognize whom it is we worship. We have to get it right at the outset.

Do we understand that God is **the Ultimate Measure?** It isn't about us; it's about Him.

Do we understand that God is **the Ultimate Treasure?** We must come to the point where we can honestly say with the psalmist, *"Whom have I in heaven but You, and there is nothing on earth that I desire besides You."* If we don't have God and have everything, we end up with nothing. If we have nothing, but God, we end up with everything.

And do we understand that God is **the Ultimate Pleasure**, that at His right hand *"there are pleasures forever more?"*

We can make Him Lord and King of our lives only as we use these first 2 verses as a jumping off place, a launching pad, as it were.

Next, He is …

King of My Life.

"Who may ascend the hill of the LORD? Who may stand in his holy place?" (v 3).

As believers, we know that we twice belong to the Lord, by right of creation and by right of redemption. Our Lord, by His precious blood, has paid the redemption price and bought and brought us out of the slave market of sin and set us free. Therefore, we owe Him our undivided love and loyalty, because we are His in a double sense. How should we respond? How should we approach Him?

David suggests that we should approach Him each day in this way. *"He who has clean hands and a pure heart, who does not lift up his soul to an idol (vanity) or swear by what is false" (v 4).*

1. With clean hands—**outwardly** keeping self from the defilement of the world.

2. With a pure heart—**inwardly** with singleness of motive and desire.

3. With undivided love and loyalty—**upwardly** with no competing loyalties in life. *"Not lifting one's soul unto vanity"*—We either lift up our soul to the Lord, or we lift it up to vanity, that which does not profit. In other words, we must allow nothing to compete.

Jesus says essentially the same thing in the beatitudes. The first three beatitudes are given to remove conflict between God and us, the second series of three remove the conflict within—us with ourselves, and the third series of three, removing the conflict between us and others.

James gives his own commentary on the teaching of our Lord in the Sermon on the Mount. He writes, *"Come near to God and he will come near to you. Wash your hands, you sinners, and purify your hearts, you double-minded"* (James 4:6-8).

We are not talking about what it takes to be saved here, but how we should respond to the God who owns us, bought us, and loves us. The Scriptures have but one answer. **What He asks is our all.** The phrase that is repeatedly used in the Old Testament is *"with all your heart and with all your soul."* The worship response from the soul of man is always "wholeheartedness" not "half-heartedness." It is underscored by Jesus in his teaching about true disciples who "leave all, forsake all, give all" for His sake. As the song puts it …

Not just a part, or half of my heart.
I will give all to Thee.

The only way we can avoid conflict within is to give Him our all, with nothing in us that competes with our love and loyalty to Him.

God takes pleasure in such a life. Such are blessed and vindicated by God.

And David suggests further in verse 6 that only those who seek the Lord with their whole heart and soul, find Him and see Him. *"Such is the generation of those who seek Him, who seek your face, O God of Jacob. Selah"* We are not seeking something for ourselves; we are seeking Him, His face, His approval.

King of my life, I crown Thee now,
Thine shall the glory be.
Lest I forget Thy thorn-crowned brow,
Lead me to Calvary.

He is not only King of the Universe, and King of My Life, but He is also

King of Glory.

"Lift up your heads, O you gates; be lifted up, you ancient doors, that the King of glory may come in" (v 7).

Those who have acknowledged Him king of their lives will one day welcome Him as King of glory. He came to Jerusalem once, and was rejected by His own people. He wept over the city,

"O Jerusalem, Jerusalem, you that kill the prophets, and stone them who are sent to you, how often would I have gathered your children together, even as a hen gathers her chicks under her wings, but you would not!"

He is coming again! Who is this king of glory? It is none other than Y'shua. He will return as King of kings and Lord of lords riding forth on His great white charger. It will be as Victor over all His enemies. The redeemed of all ages will be with Him, and join with the heavenly hosts to ascribe to Him glory, power, honor, worth, and praise. He shall establish His everlasting kingdom, and rule on David's throne.

Today the ancient gate, known as The Golden Gate is walled up. But when our Lord returns to the Mount of Olives, He will enter Jerusalem through that gate. It will not keep Him out!

Father, you are the Supreme Owner of all, and you deserve the obedience and homage of all.

The devout heart sees all things in God, and God in all things. Oh, let me see my utter need to totally depend on you, my Creator and Owner.

Augustine speaks to this, "I asked the earth; it said, I am not He; and all that therein is, made the same acknowledgment. I asked the sea and the depths, and all that move and live therein, and they answered, We are not thy God; seek higher. I asked the winds, but the air with all it inhabitants answered, I am not Thy God. I asked the heavens, the sun, the moon, the stars, and they answered, Neither are we the God whom thou seekest. And I said to all things that surrounded me, Ye have told me concerning my God, that you are not He; speak then to me of Him. And they all cried with loud voices, He made us!" (Confessions)

Things To Ponder

Throw wide your portals, Oh ye heavenly gates,
And let His ransomed train exulting pass!
Come forth! Conqueror, in Thy royal robes,
    For Thou alone
Hast triumphed o'er Thy foes; and now Thou bear'est
Upon Thy vesture and Thy thigh the name
Of King of kings. Come, then, and take Thy throne,
For Thine it is by right, too long usurped.
Thine is the kingdom, all the power is Thine
For ever; and to Thee—alone to Thee shall endless praise
And everlasting glory be ascribed!

Psalm 25

"A Model Prayer For Petition"

Psalm 25

Of David.

1 To you, O LORD, I lift up my soul;

2 in you I trust, O my God. Do not let me be put to shame,
    nor let my enemies triumph over me.

3 No one whose hope is in you will ever be put to shame,
    but they will be put to shame who are treacherous without excuse.

4 Show me your ways, O LORD,
    teach me your paths;

5 guide me in your truth and teach me,
    for you are God my Savior,
    and my hope is in you all day long.

6 Remember, O LORD, your great mercy and love,
    for they are from of old.
7 Remember not the sins of my youth and my rebellious ways;
    according to your love remember me, for you are good, O LORD.

8 Good and upright is the LORD;
    therefore he instructs sinners in his ways.

9 He guides the humble in what is right
    and teaches them his way.

10 All the ways of the LORD are loving and faithful
    for those who keep the demands of his covenant.

11 For the sake of your name, O LORD,
    forgive my iniquity, though it is great.

12 Who, then, is the man that fears the LORD?
  He will instruct him in the way chosen for him.

13 He will spend his days in prosperity,
  and his descendants will inherit the land.

14 The LORD confides in those who fear him;
  he makes his covenant known to them.

15 My eyes are ever on the LORD,
  for only he will release my feet from the snare.

16 Turn to me and be gracious to me,
  for I am lonely and afflicted.

17 The troubles of my heart have multiplied;
  free me from my anguish.

18 Look upon my affliction and my distress
  and take away all my sins.

19 See how my enemies have increased
  and how fiercely they hate me!

20 Guard my life and rescue me;
  let me not be put to shame,
  for I take refuge in you.

21 May integrity and uprightness protect me,
  because my hope is in you.

22 Redeem Israel, O God,
  from all their troubles!

NIV

Psalm 25

A Model Prayer For Petition

Note first that the psalmist's confidence rests on the character of God. He specifically mentions

1. His truth (v 5)
2. His mercy (v 6)
3. His love (v 6)
4. His goodness (v 8)
5. His righteousness (v 8)
6. His faithfulness (v 10)

With his faith firmly founded on the faithfulness and goodness of God, He proceeds to petition the Lord.

1. Deliver Me. *"Do not let me be put to shame, nor let my enemies triumph over me" (v 2)*

Positive: *"No one whose hope is in you will be put to shame."*
Negative: *"But they who are treacherous without excuse will be put to shame."*

2. Guide Me. *"He guides the humble in what is right, and teaches them in His way"*

3. Forgive Me. *"For the sake of your name, O Lord, forgive my iniquity, though it is great" (v 11).*

4. Turn To Me. *"Be gracious to me ... free me ... look on me ... take away from me ... deliver me ... guard me ... rescue me."*

Psalm 25

A Model Prayer For Petition

For some time now, I have been impressed with how different Biblical petitions are from those we usually pray. This is true in both Testaments. Often our petitions relate to such matters as the car won't start, or help in losing weight, or that a relative or friend might be helped or healed. And these requests are not wrong; they often omit mentioning the things that seem to matter most to God—that we might experience victory over sin, that our lives be a sacrifice of praise, that our actions not betray our Lord, that God's will be done on earth as it is in heaven.

As with nearly all Old Testament prayers, Psalm 25, as a prayer of petition, contains requests that are lofty and address spiritual concerns. Before we examine it more closely, it might be of interest to know that this psalm, along with Psalm 34, is in the form of an alphabetic acrostic. Both psalms contain 22 verses, and many believe they are divided in a series of three heptads or sevens ($7 \times 3 = 21$) with the concluding verse being a general petition for the redemption of the nation Israel.

I would like to use this psalm as a model prayer of petition. At the very beginning, the psalmist addresses His Lord.

O Lord, I lift up my soul to you;
O my God, I trust in you.

And the **confidence** that he has in the Lord runs like a refrain through the psalm.

I trust in you (v 1)
My hope is in you all day long (v 5)
I take refuge in you (v 20)
My hope is in you (v 21)

He makes the strong assertion in verse 3 that *"no one whose hope is in you will be put to shame!"*

This great confidence rests on the **character** of God. He specifically mentions

His truth (v 5)
His mercy (v 6)
His love (v 6)
His goodness (v 8)
His righteousness (v 8)
His faithfulness (v 10)

With his faith firmly founded on the faithfulness and goodness of his God, he proceeds to petition the Lord.

We will identify six such petitions that might serve as subjects for personal requesting.

Deliver Me.

The main request is found in verse 2, *"Do not let me be put to shame, nor let my enemies triumph over me."*

Then follows both a positive and a negative statement using the phrase *"will be put to shame."*

Positive: *"No one whose hope is in you will be put to shame."*
Negative: *"But they who are treacherous without excuse will be put to shame."*

Most of us are not surrounded by the kind of enemies that David as warrior and king had, but we must be continually aware that we are "surrounded by the enemy"—spiritual forces that are intent on our defeat and disgrace. We may well pray that we not bring shame on the name of the Lord. They are stronger than us. We need the whole armor on plus prayer to overcome them!

Next, the psalmist prays for guidance.

Guide Me.

The petition is in the form of a trio of requests:

Show me your ways, O Lord,
Teach me your paths;
Guide me in your truth and teach me.

Again the refrain of confidence comes through, *"For you are God my Savior and my hope is in you all day long"* (v 5).

Next, the psalmist asks the Lord to remember.

Remember Me.

First, David asks the Lord to remember something about His own character, *"Remember, O Lord your great mercy and love, for they are from old."* Does the Lord need to be reminded of who He is? Well, not really, but we need the assurance of His mercy and love.

Then David asks the Lord to forget certain things about his early life. *"Remember not the sins of my youth and my rebellious ways."* Does the Lord forget anything? Well, probably not, but He can **will** to forget. This means that He will never bring it up ever again. Because of the sacrifice of our Lord in bearing our sins on himself, God forgives and forgets. The author of Hebrews quotes from Jeremiah in chapter 10 verse 17, *"Their sins and lawless acts I will remember no more!"*

Then the psalmist asks, *"Remember me according to your love,"* and then adds, *"for you are good, O Lord" (v 7).*

Indeed, He is good to provide a way out of our sin-bound state and back into His holy presence!

He goes on to pursue that thought a little further … that God is good. *"Good and upright is the Lord."* and because of this, He not only doesn't remember our sin any longer, but helps us walk in His way or keep from sinning.

> *He instructs sinners in His ways.*
> *He guides the humble in what is right, and*
> *He teaches them in His way.*

How does He do this? Obviously, through His will as revealed in His Word.

The psalmist's next petition logically follows what he has just said. He asks that the Lord to forgive him.

Forgive Me.

"For the sake of your name, O Lord, forgive my iniquity, though it is great" (v 11). I wonder if we understand the enormity of our offenses against a holy God? Do we see ourselves as "great" sinners? If we do, then we magnify the grace of God in forgiving us our sins.

The psalmist then asks the question …*"Who, then, is the man that fears the Lord?" (v 12).*

God will do some wonderful things for the one who reverences Him.

He will instruct him in the way chosen for him.
He will prosper him. *He will spend his days in prosperity,*
    and his descendants will inherit the land.
He will confide in him. *He makes His covenant known to them.*

He concludes this thought by saying, *"My eyes are ever on the Lord, for only He will release my feet from the snare." (v 15).* That constitutes the proper focus in life … "Look to Jesus …" David has one more petition—actually a series of petitions that pour out of his heart. He prays …

Turn To Me.

Please notice my predicament! I need you to see me through this. The words expressing his difficulties are very expressive: "lonely," "afflicted," "troubles," "anguish," "distress," "sin," "enemies." So his petitions are urgent.

"Be gracious to me … free me … look on me … take away from me … deliver me … guard me … rescue me."

And he includes that confident refrain at this point, *"For I take refuge in you." (v 20)*

Where can I go but to the Lord? When I'm lonely and afflicted and troubled, in anguish and distress, with the sense of failure weighing heavily on me, with my foes fiercely opposing me—**I take refuge in you, O Lord!**

He closes the song with a final personal appeal. *"May integrity and uprightness protect me"* and then another confident assertion, *"Because my hope is in you" (v 21).*

And one final general appeal, that seems almost unrelated to what has gone before, except that he recognizes his solidarity with the people of God, *"Redeem Israel, O God, from all their troubles!" (v 22).*

> *"Father, like the psalmist, I find myself fleeing to the only refuge I have in times of distress—to You! And I pour out my soul in earnest prayer that you would rescue me, and bring me out! "My hope is in you, Lord! Yes, where could I go, but to the Lord?*

Things To Ponder

Note, the psalmist assumes that God is mindful of what he is facing, and will come in answer to his earnest petition, and bring him out of his distress. Do we share his confidence?

Psalm 26

"Loving The Place Where God's Glory Dwells"

Psalm 26

Of David.

1 Vindicate me, O LORD, for I have led a blameless life;
    I have trusted in the LORD without wavering.

2 Test me, O LORD, and try me,
    examine my heart and my mind;

3 for your love is ever before me,
    and I walk continually in your truth.

4 I do not sit with deceitful men,
    nor do I consort with hypocrites;

5 I abhor the assembly of evildoers
    and refuse to sit with the wicked.

6 I wash my hands in innocence,
    and go about your altar, O LORD,

7 proclaiming aloud your praise
    and telling of all your wonderful deeds.

8 I love the house where you live, O LORD,
    the place where your glory dwells.

9. Do not take away my soul along with sinners,
    my life with bloodthirsty men,

10 in whose hands are wicked schemes,
    whose right hands are full of bribes.

11 But I lead a blameless life;
    redeem me and be merciful to me.

12 My feet stand on level ground;
   in the great assembly I will praise the LORD.

NIV

Psalm 26

"Loving The Place Where God's Glory Dwells"

David's heart was in the right place …

I. A Whole Heart. *"Vindicate me, O LORD,"*

A. I have lived for you without reservation. *"I have lead a blameless life"* *(a life of integrity, wholeheartedness)*
B. I have trusted you without wavering (I shall not slip—doubt v 1)

II. A Pure Heart. *"Test me, O LORD, and try me (prove me) examine my heart (motives) and my mind" (v 2).*

A. Positively: This is what you will find.

1. **Your love fills my vision.** *"Your love (kindness) is ever before me (before my eyes)" (v 3).*
2. **Your truth shapes my life.** *"I walk continually (to and fro) in your truth." (v 3).*

B. Negatively: I hate the company of evil men.

1. I do not sit with deceitful men. *"I do not consort with hypocrites" (v 4)*
2. I abhor the assembly of evildoers. *"I refuse to sit with the wicked (the lawless) (v 5)*

"Don't take away my soul along with sinners,
        my life with bloodthirsty men (v 9).
In whose hands are wicked schemes,
        Whose right hands are full of bribes (v 10).

III. A Dedicated Heart.

A. *"I wash (laver) my hands (palms) in innocence, and go (march) about your altar (the altar of burnt offering), O LORD" (V 6).*
B. *"Proclaiming aloud our praise, and telling of all your wonderful deeds (v 7).*
C. *I love the house where you live, O LORD, the place where your glory dwells (v 8).*

IV. A Steadfast Heart. *"Redeem me, and be merciful to me" (v 11).*

A. I (will) lead a blameless life (a life of integrity) (v 1)
B. My feet stand on level ground.
C. In the great assembly (congregation), I will praise the LORD (V 12)

Psalm 26

"Loving The Place Where God's Glory Dwells"

Psalm 26, 27, and 28 all mention the dwelling place of God, a a reference to the Holy of holies, the innermost room of the tabernacle where God's presence was localized in the midst of His people. There the 'Shekinah' blazed between the outstretched arms of the cherubim, and there the people came, in their representative High Priest, where the atoning blood gave the only access into God's holy presence. Today, because of Christ's atoning sacrifice, and the rent veil of his flesh, we may come and find grace to help in time of need. That inner room of holiness is found replicated in our hearts, and God is there to meet with us when we come. What a privilege that is! Be reminded of Paul's words to the Corinthians, *"Do you not know that your body is a temple of the Holy Spirit, who is in you, whom you have received from God? You are not your own; you were bought at a price. Therefore honor God with your body"* (I Corinthians 6:19-20).

To David, the tabernacle of meeting was the place where he could be close to God, a place of protection from his enemies, and a place where he could direct his petitions, and wait for God's answer. So the central theme of this psalm can be found in verse 8.

> *I love the house where you live, O Lord,*
> *The place where your glory dwells.*

David knew that it is an awesome experience to come into the presence of God. Yea, it is a searching experience. That's how David begins this psalm, by actually calling on God to vindicate him, to test and prove him in the deepest recesses of his heart. What a courageous thing to ask! Who of us would dare to ask God for such a thing? Certainly David was wholehearted.

A Whole Heart

> *"Vindicate me, O LORD, for I have lead a blameless life; I have trusted in the LORD with out wavering" (v 1).*

David said to Saul on one occasion. "May the Lord judge between you and me. And may the Lord avenge the wrongs you have done to me, but my hand will not touch you" (I Sam. 24:12).

His words claiming blamelessness sound a bit strange to our ears, but they shouldn't. The words are no boast. He is not claiming moral perfection, but uprightness of heart.

Paul admonishes believers to live blameless lives. He writes to the Ephesians and says, "(God) chose us in him before the creation of the world to be holy and blameless in his sight" (1:4). He goes on, of course to tell us that such a life is made possible through the redemption that is in Christ. Or be reminded of his word to the Philippians, "That you may become blameless and pure, children of God without fault in a crooked and depraved generation, in which you shine like stars in the universe" (2:15-16).

David says two remarkable things here about himself.

1. **I have lived for you wholeheartedly.** When he says that he has lived a blameless life or a life of integrity, he is not saying that he has lived a sinless life. Integrity implies wholeness, a life that is not divided or conflicted. He was single minded and wholehearted in his devotion to the Lord. And still further, he asserts ...

2. **I have trusted you without wavering or doubting.** He was not like the man that James describes, a man of duplicity. *"who doubts and is like the wave of the sea, blown and tossed by the wind"* (1:60. David has no doubts about His God. He knew Him to be faithful and true to His promises. The Judge of all the earth could not but do right.

David goes on to ask God's examination of his heart and motives be thorough. It seems like a bold move on David's part. Surely he must know that God knows his heart better than he knows it.

A Pure Heart.

> *"Test me, O LORD, and try me, examine my heart (reins, kidneys) and my mind"* (v 2).

David's reference here seems to be to the methods by which metals were tested. As gold and silver were tied in the furnace so he was ready to be tried. *'The firing pot is for silver and the furnace for gold, but the Lord tries the heart"* (Proverbs 17:3). And David believes that

God will see that his inmost motives and desires are pure. He mentions two things that enable this to be so.

1. **Your love fills all my vision.** *"For your love is ever before me ..."* How often in his life had David been the recipient of God's loving kindness. Even in difficult times, or especially in difficult times, he had experienced the nearness of His Lord. It is what kept him going in his darkest night.

2. **Your truth shapes all my life.** *"and I walk continually in your truth" (v 3).* This principle regulated his life. Later David is to write *"I seek you with all my heart; do not let me stray from your commands. I have hidden your word in my heart that I might not sin against you" (119:10-11).*

A Dedicated Heart.

"I do not sit with deceitful men, nor do I consort with hypocrites; I abhor the assembly of evildoers and refuse to sit with the wicked" (v 4-5).

The saying goes "a person is known by the company he keeps." David is the man he describes in Psalm 1, the man who doesn't sit, walk, or stand with the wicked; the man who doesn't accept the world's advice or approve of the world's actions, or adopt the world's attitudes. He knows the wicked will be judged, and he doesn't want to be numbered with them (or taken away to destruction v 9). *"Do not take away my soul along with sinners ..." (v 9-10).*

On the other hand, David enjoys the company of the righteous who go to the tabernacle to commune with God. He figuratively takes the place of the priest and washes his hands at the laver (Exodus 30:17-21). He walks around and around the altar and sees the blood on its base, and the blood on each of the four hours, beholds the smoke of the fire, notes the innocent victims who have been offered there, and he gives joyful thanks for the salvation provided for him by God. *"I wash my hands in innocence, and go about your altar, O Lord, proclaiming aloud your praise and telling of all your wonderful deeds" (v 6-7).*

A Steadfast Heart.

David concludes by saying that he will steadfastly persist on this path. He changes the tense (as Kidner suggests) from 'I have walked' to 'I (will) walk'. He recognizes he cannot do this without assistance from God (redeem me, be gracious to me). His faith is firmly placed and his feet are securely planted on level ground. He joins with the congregation of the faithful in praise to the Lord.

Father, it is a solemn thing to stand before an earthly judge, but it is a far more solemn thing to come before the judgment-seat of God. This is the court of last resort. Here the Judge is personally acquainted with all the facts and circumstances of the case, and His judgments are absolutely just and final. I know that I am in the presence of the great Searcher of hearts. I pray, like David, that I have walked in integrity of heart, and have trusted in the Lord. It is the only thing that can keep me from sliding. The deepest desire of David's heart was to do right. It is my deep desire as well. As the Great Refiner, purge away my sin, and let the true and the good remain.

Things To Ponder

David here declares his love for God's house and worship. Instead of consorting with the wicked, his delight was the people of God.

Psalm 27

"Confidence In The Lord In Fearful Times"

Psalm 27

Of David.

1 The LORD is my light and my salvation—whom shall I fear?
    The LORD is the stronghold of my life—of whom shall I be afraid?

2 When evil men advance against me to devour my flesh,
    when my enemies and my foes attack me,
    they will stumble and fall.

3 Though an army besiege me, my heart will not fear;
    though war break out against me,
    even then will I be confident.

4 One thing I ask of the LORD, this is what I seek:
    that I may dwell in the house of the LORD all the days of my life,
    to gaze upon the beauty of the LORD
    and to seek him in his temple.

5 For in the day of trouble he will keep me safe in his dwelling;
    he will hide me in the shelter of his tabernacle
    and set me high upon a rock.

6 Then my head will be exalted above the enemies who surround me;
    at his tabernacle will I sacrifice with shouts of joy;
    I will sing and make music to the LORD.

7 Hear my voice when I call, O LORD;
    be merciful to me and answer me.

8 My heart says of you, "Seek his face!"
    Your face, LORD, I will seek.

9 Do not hide your face from me,
    do not turn your servant away in anger; you have been my helper.
    Do not reject me or forsake me, O God my Savior.

10 Though my father and mother forsake me,
   the LORD will receive me.

11 Teach me your way, O LORD;
   lead me in a straight path because of my oppressors.

12 Do not turn me over to the desire of my foes,
   for false witnesses rise up against me, breathing out violence.

13 I am still confident of this:
   I will see the goodness of the LORD in the land of the living.
14 Wait for the LORD;
   be strong and take heart and wait for the LORD.

NIV

Psalm 27

Confidence In The Lord In Fearful Times

I.His Confidence In The Lord.

A. The Unchangeable Object Of His Confidence.

1. The Lord is his Light—direction, guidance. *"The Lord is my light"*
2. The Lord is his Salvation—deliverance. *"The Lord is my salvation"*
3. The Lord is his Stronghold—protection. *"The Lord is the stronghold of my life" (v 1).*

His Confidence—*"whom shall I fear?" "of whom shall I be afraid?"*

B. The Unshakeable Nature of His Confidence. God has done it before; He can do it again. Confidence comes through experience.

1. Though wicked men advance against him and attack him (v 2).
2. Though an army besiege him, and war breaks out against him (v 3).

His Confidence—"they will stumble and fall" "even then will I be confident"

II.His Communion With The Lord.

A. The Purpose of Communion. *"One thing I ask (desire) of the LORD, this is what I seek" (v 4).*

1. He desired to bask in the Lord's glory. *"that I may dwell in the house of the Lord all the days of my life"*
2. He wanted to grasp the Lord's goodness. *"to gaze upon the beauty of the Lord (marvel at His goodness) (v 4)*
3. He purposed to ask the Lord's guidance. *"to seek him (inquire of Him) in his temple. (v 4).*

B. The Place of Communion.

1. The place of serenity. *"the stronghold of my life—of whom shall I fear"*
2. The place of security. *"in the day of trouble he will keep me safe in his dwelling; he will hide me in the shelter of his tabernacle" (v 5)*
3. The place of stability. *"and set me high upon a rock"(v 5)*
4. The place of victory. *Then my head will be exalted above the enemies who surround me;" (v 6)*
5. The place of joviality. *"at his tabernacle will I sacrifice with shouts of joy; I will sing and make music to the Lord." (v 6).*

IV. The Communication To The Lord.

A. **His Calling Voice** *"Hear my voice when I call, O LORD; be merciful to me and answer me" (v 7)*

B. **His Seeking Heart.** *"My heart says of you, 'Seek his face! Your face, LORD, I will seek" (v 8)*

C. **His Greatest Fear.** *"Do not hide your face from me, do not turn your servant away in anger; you have been my helper. Do not reject me or forsake me, O God my Savior. Though my father and mother forsake me, the LORD will receive me" (v 9-10).*

V. He Reaffirms His Confidence in the Lord.

"I am confident of this: I will see the goodness of the LORD in the land of the living" (v 13).

Psalm 27

Confidence In he Lord In Fearful Times

In many of the psalms that bear his name, David is in danger, surrounded by foes bent on his destruction. He was a warrior-king. We're not sure what the circumstances were here in Psalm 27, but it certainly fits the time David was fleeing for his life before Saul and his army. In I Samuel 22, David receive help from Ahimelech the priest at Nob., and Doeg, the Edomite happened to be there, saw David, and latter reported the incident to Saul. Ahimelech and his family paid dearly for assisting David. Saul destroyed them, and the whole village population where they lived. David, knowing his situation was perilous, had made provision for his parents to be protected by the king of Moab. It is understandable, therefore, that David feels abandoned (verses s9-10). But, as usual, when there is nowhere else he can find shelter, he flees to the Lord, and is unafraid.

His Confidence In The Lord.

David was confident that the Lord who had helped him before, would help him now, and in the future. So he begins with this confident assertion.

The Unchangeable Object Of His Confidence.

The Lord is his Light, giving him guidance in the way he should take. *"The Lord is my light …"* The Lord is his Salvation, granting deliverance from his enemies. *("The LORD) is my salvation …"* The Lord is his Stronghold, offering protection from his foes. *"The LORD is the stronghold of my life."* And because of this, he was unafraid. *"Whom shall I fear? Of whom shall I be afraid?"*

The Unshakeable Nature Of His Confidence.

His confidence stemmed from the Lord's intervention in his behalf in the past when confronted by evil men bent on his destruction. *"They will stumble and fall" (v 2).* And he believed that even in the future though an army come against him, and engage him in battle, they would not succeed. He refuses to be afraid, because his confidence is in the Lord! Confidence, someone has said, is the child of experience. *"My heart will not fear; I will be confident" (v 3).*

When faced with fearful prospects, is our confidence in the Lord, and can we believe that he is with us and for us in our time of need?

I will not be afraid.
What can man do to me? (Hebrews 13:6; Psalm 118: l6, 7).

Next he speaks of his desire to commune with the Lord.

His Communion With The Lord

The Purpose Of Communion

"One thing I ask (desire) of the LORD, this is what I seek …" (v 4). It is a good thing not to be scattered in our desires, but focused. Paul said, *"This one thing I do …"* Jesus said, "Seek first the kingdom of God and His righteousness.…" When God is our chief ambition, in life, then the greater will integrate the lesser. *"All these things will be yours as well."* David knew that to be true. Rather than one thing, it seems like he is asking for three things, but they are really the same desire—that he might be near the Lord. He desires to bask in the Lord's glory *"That I may dwell in the house of the Lord all the days of my life"* (v 4). He wanted to grasp the Lord's goodness *"to gaze upon the beauty (loveliness) of the Lord (marvel at His goodness)."* And he purposed to ask the Lord's guidance *"and to seek (inquire of him) in his temple" (v 4).*

The Place of Communion.

It is variously described by David as *"the house of the LORD", His temple", His dwelling", "the shelter of His tabernacle," "His tabernacle."* It is the place where God dwelled in the midst of His people. The cloud by day and the pillar of fire by night signaled the presence of the Lord to protect, provide, and guide the people in their wilderness journey. It was to David …
1. The place serenity—*"the stronghold of my life—of whim shall I fear"*
2. The place of security—*"in the day of trouble he will keep me safe in his dwelling; he will hide me in the shelter of his tabernacle."*
3. The place of stability—*"and set me upon a rock" (v 5)*
4. The place of victory—*"then my head will be exalted above the enemies who surround me"*

5. The place of joviality—"At his tabernacle will I sacrifice with shouts of joy; I will sing and make music to the LORD."

The songwriter has captured the thought well …

In the secret of His presence how my soul delights to hide!
Oh, how precious are the lessons that I learn at Jesus' side!
Earthly care can never vex me, neither trials lay me low;
For when Satan comes to tempt me, to the secret place I go.
To the secret place of I go.

When my soul is faint and thirsty, 'neath the shadow of His wing
There is cool and pleasant shelter, and a fresh and crystal spring;
And my Savior rests beside me, as we hold communion sweet:
If I tried, I could not utter what He says when thus we meet,
What He says when thus we meet.

His communion issues in communication—a prayer that has as its main theme the desire that he never be forsaken by the Lord, or all would be lost.

The Communication To The Lord.

His Calling Voice.

"Hear my voice when I call, O LORD; be merciful to me and answer me" (v 7). He wants to be assured that the Lord is listening when he calls. He waits for God's gracious answer to come. Spurgeon suggests that we should expect answered from the Lord in the same way we expect a reply to a letter of importance written to a friend.

His Seeking Heart.

"My heart says of you, 'Seek his face!' Your face, LORD, I will seek" (v 8). This is translated sometimes as a command from the Lord himself, *"When You said, Seek my face …"* Coming from the Lord, it certainly would carry more weight. Note how prompt he was to respond, "Your face, LORD, I will seek." He was seeking approval from the Lord—a smile.

His Greatest Fear.

"Do not hide your face from me, do not turn your servant away in anger; you have been my helper. Do not reject me or forsake me, O God my Savior. Though my father and mother forsake me, the LORD will receive me" (v 9-10).

"Teach me your way, OLORD; lead me in a straight path because of my oppressors. Do not turn me over to the desire of my foes, for false witnesses rise up against me, breathing out violence" (v 11-12).

His earnest prayer is that the Lord would teach him His way, and keep him on the right path. His enemies might seek to get him off track; slander his name, and do harm to his person, but if he pleased the Lord that was his chief desire. If the Lord saw him at his best, let his enemies do their worst!

So his final admonition is a word reaffirming his confidence in the Lord.

He Reaffirms His Confidence In The Lord.

"I am confident of this: I will see the goodness of the LORD in the land of the living" (v 13).

In effect, David says, "Don't try to work it out on our own. Don't rush ahead of th4e Lord.
Don't be impatient. *"Wait for the Lord: be strong and take heart. Wait for the Lord!" (v 14)* The Lord's timing may not be ours, but we can afford to wait. We can remain strong and confident that He is working all things out after the counsel of His own will, and for our good.

> *"Father, I am reminded of what David writes elsewhere. 'Then my enemies will turn back when I call for help. By this I will know that God is for me" (56:9).* But the apostle Paul gives us a far greater assurance when he says, *"If God be for us, who can be against us? He who did not spare his own Son, but gave him up for us all—how will he not also, along with him, graciously give us all things?"(Romans 8:31-32). How can we ever doubt that you are for us when you have proven it by giving your One and Only Son to die for us! Thank you for the confidence we can have that along with Him you give us all else besides.*

Things To Ponder

Consider David's experience of seeking the Lord in "His temple" as finding its counterpart in the wonderful privilege every child of God has of *"drawing near to God with a sincere heart in full assurance of faith."* The author of Hebrews (10:19-20) says that we can enter the Most Holy Place with confidence *"by the blood of Jesus, by a new and living way opened for us through the curtain, that is, his body (flesh) …"*

Psalm 28

"A Cry For Help"

Psalm 28

Of David.

1 To you I call, O LORD my Rock;
    do not turn a deaf ear to me.
For if you remain silent,
    I will be like those who have gone down to the pit.

2 Hear my cry for mercy as I call to you for help,
    as I lift up my hands toward your Most Holy Place.

3 Do not drag me away with the wicked,
    with those who do evil,
    who speak cordially with their neighbors but harbor malice in their
    hearts.

4 Repay them for their deeds and for their evil work;
    repay them for what their hands have done
    and bring back upon them what they deserve.

5 Since they show no regard for the works of the LORD
    and what his hands have done,
    he will tear them down and never build them up again.

6 Praise be to the LORD,
    for he has heard my cry for mercy.

7 The LORD is my strength and my shield;
    my heart trusts in him, and I am helped.
    My heart leaps for joy and I will give thanks to him in song.

8 The LORD is the strength of his people,
    a fortress of salvation for his anointed one.

9 Save your people and bless your inheritance;
    be their shepherd and carry them forever.

NIV

Psalm 28

A Cry For Help

I. Plea For Mercy Uttered. *"hear my cry for mercy as I call to you for help." (v 2)*

A. The Plea is to the God of Mercy. *"To you I call, O LORD my Rock ..." (v 1).*
B. His Plea is to the Place of Mercy, the Mercy Seat. *"... as I lift up my hands toward your Most Holy Place (v 2)*
C. The substance of his plea. *"Don't treat me as you do the wicked. "Do not drag (draw) me away with the wicked" (v 3).*

1. They practice iniquity. "those who do evil" (v 3).
2. They engage in duplicity. "those who speak cordially with their neighbors but harbor malice in their hearts" (v 3).
3. Reciprocity. "Repay them ... repay them ... bring back upon them what they deserve (v 4)
4. Intractability. "Since they show no regard for the works of the LORD, and what His hands have done, he will tear them down, and never build them up again (v 5).

II. Praise for Mercy Rendered. *"Praise be to the LORD,` for he has heard my cry for mercy" (v 6).*

A. His Trust in the Lord. *"The Lord is my strength and my shield; my heart trusts in him, and I am helped."*

1. My strength
2. My shield

B. His Joy in the Lord. *"My heart leaps for joy and I will give thanks to him in song" (v7).*

III. Prayer for the People.

A. Lord, You Are Their Stronghold. *"The Lord is the strength of his people, a fortress of salvation for his anointed one" (v 8).*

B. Lord, Be Their Shepherd. *"Save your people and bless your inheritance: be their shepherd and carry them forever" (v 9).*

1. Save them.
2. Bless them.
3. Carry them.

Psalm 28

A Cry For Help

In Psalm 27 we are admonished to wait for the Lord, and anticipate His answer. Psalm l28 seems to be a sequel to Psalm 27. Is prayer always answered immediately? Obviously not, because God's timing is better than ours.

His Plea For Mercy Uttered

"To you I call, O Lord my Rock; do not turn a deaf ear to me" (v 1). "Hear my cry for mercy as I call to you for help" (v 2).

David here is obviously uttering a cry for help. It appears to be a cry of desperation, because he twice repeats it, "Do not turn a deaf ear ... Hear my cry." We're not sure what his plight was. The matter of greatest importance is that he knows where to go to find help. Jesus stressed that we should always pray and not give up (Luke 18:1). Be persistent, like David, and don't lose heart.

His Pleas Directed To The **God** of Mercy

He pleads with the God of all mercy who is his Rock—the One on whom he can rely, the One who keeps him steady when everything else is shaking. A wife may say of her husband, "He' my rock!", and she means that he is steady, that he is there for her to lean on, and from whom she draws her strength. In s much greater sense, the Lord is all of that and more to us!

But David expresses concern that his request seems to have fallen on deaf ears. The voice of the Lord can sometimes be terrible, like a gathering thunderstorm (Psalm 29), but when there is no response, only silence, the effect can be equally devastating. The psalmist knows that his God answers prayer, but where are the answers? If the answer does not come, then his plight is no different from those who are separated from God in Sheol. Without an answer from God, he would be like a dead man! He must have an answer. *"I will be like those who have gone down to the pit."*

His Plea Directed To the **Place** of Mercy, the Mercy Seat. *"I call to you for help as I lift up my hands toward your Most Holy Place (Oracle)" (v 2).*

He lifts up his hands, eager and expectant to receive what God might give, and he directs the prayer to "your Most Holy Place" a reference to the Holy of Holies where the Ark of the Covenant was, and The Mercy Seat (God's Throne) where, with the Atoning Sacrifice, the saints go to *"find grace to help in time of need"* (Heb. 4:16). I wonder if we are equally insistent on answers to prayer? And are we mindful of the answer when it comes?

Don't Treat Me As You Would The Wicked

He did not want to be included along with the wicked when they are brought to justice. God doesn't answer the prayer of the wicked, And David does not want to be "bundled" with them. *"Do not drag me away with the wicked"* as a prisoner is dragged away to punishment.

The wicked …

Practice **iniquity**. *"those who do evil."* They are "workers" of iniquity.
Engage in **duplicity**. *"Those who speak cordially with their neighbors but harbor malice in their hearts"* (v 3).
Deserve **reciprocity**, pay back. *"Repay them … repay them for what their hands have done, and bring back upon them what they deserve"* (v 4). Treat them as they treat others.
The psalmist contrasts the works of the wicked, and what their hands have done, with the works of the LORD, and what His hands have done. *"Since they show no regard for the works of the LORD, and what His hands have done …"* (v 5). They will not succeed in what they do, but will be torn down, rather than being built up. David is not being vindictive here, but insisting that justice be done, and that the wicked experience fully the wrath of God that they deserve.

Praise For Mercy Rendered. *"Praise be to the LORD, for he has heard my cry for mercy"* (v 6).

David's prayer for mercy is heard! His first reaction is to praise the Lord. Does God answer prayer? Yes! Then we must be alert to the answer when it comes, and offer Him our grateful thanks.

His Trust In The Lord.

"The LORD is my strength and my shield; my heart trusts in him, and I am helped." Is God our Rock? Is God trustworthy? Of course. He is my inward

strength, and my outward shield. He provides for me and protects me, and invariably helps me when I call. We're not always sure what God is up to, but we can be sure that He desires our highest good.

His Joy In The Lord.

Note with what exuberance David expresses himself, *"My heart leaps for joy and I will give thanks to him in song" (v 7)*. The inward joy finds outward expression in thankful song.

Prayer For The People Offered.

Lord, You Are Their Strength!

Not only does David recognize that the Lord is his strength and shield, but He is also *"the strength of his people."* David as the "anointed" of God is, of course, a type of Messiah, The Anointed of God (The Christ).

Lord, Be Their Shepherd!

God's people are His inheritance, His most valuable possession! He shepherds them, and as their Shepherd, He even carries them, Isaiah puts it so beautifully, *"He tends his flock like a shepherd; He gathers the lambs in his arms and carries them close to his heart; he gently leads those that have young" (40:11)*. In Isaiah 46:1-7, the prophet draws a contrast between the people carrying their gods which are "a heavy burden", and God carrying His people form birth to the grave, *"I have made you and I will carry you; I will sustain you and I will rescue you."*

> *Father, it is good to be reminded that you do answer our cries for help, even though it sometimes seems like you are silent. Help us to continue to trust you, and this because you are always trustworthy. We are the sheep of your pasture, and you are mindful that we often go astray or hurt ourselves by our wrong choices. We often get so tired, Lord. Please reach down and lift us up, and hold us close.*

Things To Ponder

In Ephesians 1:18, the apostle speaks of the riches of God's "glorious inheritance in the saints." This could mean either God's inheritance or ours, either the inheritance he receives or the inheritance he bestows. The parallel passage in Colossians 1:12 suggests that 'God's inheritance" refers to what he will give us, for we are to give thanks to the Father *"who has qualified us to share in the inheritance of the saints in light* (J. Stott, *God's New Society*, p. 56). Either way, we are rich indeed!

Psalm 29

"The Thundering Voice of Yahweh"

Psalm 29

A psalm of David

1 Ascribe (give) to **the LORD,** O mighty ones,
　　Ascribe to the Lord glory and strength.
2 Ascribe to **the LORD** the glory due his name;
　　worship (bow down before) the LORD in the splendor of his holiness.

3 **The voice of the LORD** is over the waters;
　　　the God of glory thunders,
　　　the LORD thunders over the mighty waters.
4 **The voice of the LORD** is powerful;
　　　the voice of **the LORD** is majestic.
5 **The voice of the LORD** breaks the cedars;
　　　the LORD breaks in pieces the cedars of Lebanon.
6 He makes Lebanon skip like a calf,
　　　Sirion like a young wild ox.
7 **The voice of the LORD** strikes with flashes of lightning.
8 **The voice of the LORD** shakes (whirls) the desert;
　　　the LORD shakes the Desert of Kadesh.
9 **The voice of the LORD** twists the oaks
　　　and strips the forests bare.

And in his temple all cry, "Glory!"

10 **The LORD** sits enthroned over the flood;
　　　the LORD is enthroned as King forever.
11 **The LORD** gives strength to his people;
　　　the LORD blesses his people with peace.

NIV

Psalm 29

The Thundering Voice of The Lord

I. The Might And Majesty of the Lord Praised. *"Ascribe to Lord the glory due His name …"*

A. The angelic hosts praise Yahweh for His glory and strength. *"Ascribe to the Lord, O mighty ones …" (v 1)*
B. They bow before Him and cry "holy, holy, holy." *"… worship the Lord in the splendor (beauty) of his holiness." (v 2)*

II. The Mighty And Majestic Voice Of the Lord Is Heard In The Gathering Storm.

A. The Storm begins at sea on the Mediterranean. *"The voice of the Lord is over the mighty waters. The voice of the Lord thunders over mighty waters" (v 3).*
B. The Storm gains in intensity as it moves inland over Lebanon to the north. *"The voice of the Lord is powerful; the voice of the Lord is majestic. The voice of The Lord breaks the cedars; The Lord breaks in pieces the cedars of Lebanon. He makes Lebanon skip like a calf, Sirion like a young wild ox" (v 5, 6).*
C. The Storm sweeps to the south over the desert wilderness. *"The voice of the Lord strikes with flashes of lightning. The voice of the Lord shakes (whirls) the desert; The Lord shakes the Desert of Kadesh. The voice of the Lord twists the oaks and strips the forests bare (v 7-9).*

"And in His temple all cry, "Glory!"

III. This Powerful And Majestic God Is Personal.

A. He is enthroned forever. *"The voice of the Lord sits enthroned over the flood; The Lord is enthroned as King forever" (v 10).*
B. He watches over his people, granting them strength and blessing them with peace. *"The Lord gives strength to his people; Yahweh blesses his people with peace" (v 11).*

Psalm 29

The Thundering Voice of Yahweh

A Psalm used at the Feast of Tabernacles (Lev. 23:36) commemorating Israel's journey through the wilderness; and also at The Feast of Pentecost (Talmud).

I live on the Central Coast of California in Monterey, and I vividly remember one night several years ago, witnessing from our living room window that overlooks Monterey Bay, a magnificent display of God's pyrotechnics. Lightning lit up the sky followed by deep rumblings of thunder and occasionally a crackling sound as if the heavens were splitting open. It was awesome! I recalled Job's description of a thunderstorm. Job cries out in excitement and wonder, *"Listen! Listen to the roar of his voice, to the rumbling that comes from his mouth" (37:1)*. He graphically describes the thunder and lightning storm.

> Who can understand how he spreads out the clouds,
>   how he thunders from his pavilion?
> See how he scatters the lightning about him,
>   bathing the depth of the sea.
> This is the way he governs the nations
>   and provides food in abundance.
> He fills his hands with lightning
>   and commands it to strike its mark.
> His thunder announces the coming storm;
>   even the cattle make known its approach.
> At this my heart pounds and leaps from its place.
> Listen! Listen to the roar of his voice,
>   to the rumbling that comes from his mouth.
> He unleashes his lightning beneath the whole heaven
>   and sends it to the ends of the earth.
> After that comes the sound of his roar;
>   he thunders in marvelous ways;
>   he does great things beyond our understanding."

Moses and the people trembled at the presence of God when the Law was given on Mt Sinai, *"On the morning of the third day there was thunder and lightning, with a thick cloud over the mountain, and a very loud trumpet blast. Everyone in the camp trembled" (Exodus 19:16).* The author of Hebrews alludes to the *"darkness, gloom and storm"* that surrounded the mount that could not be touched on penalty of death. And the apostle John on Patmos was caught up *"in the Spirit"* to heaven, and one of the indicators of God's presence on the throne is given: *" flashes of lightning, rumblings and peals of thunder" (Rev. 4:5).*

It is little wonder, therefore, that David's graphic description of a thunderstorm in Psalm 29 begins in heaven with the angels praising the might and majesty of God. It is as if the thunder and lightning that surrounds his throne sweep to earth, and Nature becomes the mouthpiece of deity. Are thunder utterances intelligible? They are when God wants them to be! In Revelation chapter 10, Seven Thunders spoke, but John was prohibited from transcribing their message

> *"When he (the Mighty Angel) shouted, the voices of the seven thunders spoke. And when the seven thunders spoke, I was about to write; but I heard a voice from heaven say, 'Seal up what the seven thunders have said and do not write it down" (v 3-4).*

We are not told what they uttered, and little can be gained by conjecture. There is probably no direct connection between Revelation 10 and Psalm 29, but it is interesting that David here mentions seven thunder-voices of Yahweh speaking through the tempest. It was a storm that moved swiftly in from the Mediterranean Sea, gaining in velocity as it swept inland over Lebanon to the north, then traveled rapidly down the length of Palestine in hurricane-like destructiveness, and finally exhausted itself in the desert wilderness of Kadesh to the south. David saw in the storm the might and majesty of Yahweh.

The Might And Majesty of Yahweh Praised.

"Ascribe (give) to the LORD, O mighty ones. Ascribe to the LORD glory and strength. Ascribe to the LORD the glory due his name; worship the LORD in (for) the splendor of his holiness" (v 1, 2).

This is a summons to the angels (elim) to give God his due. The seraphim in Isaiah 6:3 also ascribe to the LORD "glory and holiness". Kidner suggests that "holy" speaks of what God is, and 'glory' of all that proceeds from Him (*Psalms*

1-72, page 125). In Psalm 96:9, where the latter phrase is repeated, the worshipers are *"all the people of the earth."* Certainly, He is worthy of universal praise!

The Mighty and Majestic Voice of Yahweh Heard in The Gathering Storm.

A. The Storm begins at sea. *"The voice of the Lord is over the mighty waters. The voice of the LORD thunders over mighty waters" (v 3).* This is undoubtedly the Mediterranean Sea. Immediately the thunder becomes the "voice" of God, not Nature's voice, but the voice of the Creator-God.

B. The Storm moves inland. *"The voice of the LORD breaks the cedars; the LORD breaks in pieces the cedars of Lebanon. He makes Lebanon skip like a calf, Sirion like a young wild ox" (v 5-6).* The tempest sweeps from Lebanon to Sirion (Mount Hermon) in the far north. The force of the wind shattered the great cedars of Lebanon. The mountain heights are no match for the stormy blasts. Isaiah 2:12ff speaks of the Day of the Lord when *cedars and mountains*, impressive in their height and strength, will be humbled (brought low) along with the arrogant pride of men.

> *"The Lord Almighty has a day in store for all the proud and lofty, for all that is exalted (and they will be humbled), for all the cedars of Lebanon, tall and lofty, and all the oaks of Bashan, for all the towering mountains and all the high hills, for every lofty tower and every forti-fied wall, for every trading ship and every stately vessel. The arrogance of man will be brought low and the pride of men humbled;* **the Lord alone will be exalted in that day,** *and the idols will totally disappear."*

(3) Then the Storm moves to the south, to Kadesh, where Israel had vacil-lated in their unbelief, and they were turned back to wander in the wilderness forty years. *"The voice of the LORD strikes with flashes of lightning (forked). The voice of the LORD shakes the desert; the LORD shakes the Desert of Kadesh. The voice of the LORD twists the oaks and strips the forests bare" (v 7-9).* The con-junction of fire and mighty wind may be the reason why the Talmud assigns this psalm to Pentecost. In Acts 2, on the Day of Pentecost, *"a violent wind from heaven … tongues of fire"* announced the descent of the Holy Spirit on the prayerful gathering in the upper room. They knew as David knew, that this awesome display was a God-Thing!

Every voice in the heavenly (and earthly) temple cry *"Glory!"* Like a child looking at fireworks, the worshipers are witnessing the awesome holiness and power of God.

The psalmist concludes the psalm by stressing that this powerful God is his personal God.

This Powerful and Majestic God is Personal.

He is enthroned as King forever. *"The voice of the LORD sits enthroned over the flood; The LORD is enthroned as King forever" (v 10)*. The word *flood* here is found elsewhere only in Genesis 6 where it is used of Noah's flood. The psalmist seems to compare what he has just witnessed with the disaster unleashed by God on Noah's contemporaries. The same powerful God who destroyed the inhabitants of the earth except eight souls, now speaks from His throne again!

But more importantly, He is the God who channels His mighty strength to work in behalf of His people. *"The LORD gives strength to his people; The LORD blesses His people with peace" (v 11)*. Only His enemies need tremble at His wrath. His own people dwell secure.

Father, certainly this psalm speaks of your might and majesty inspiring us puny men and women to prostrate ourselves in awe and wonder before You. Who dares resist You? Everything is swept away before your awesome power. You are enthroned "over the flood" and as "King forever." Your people dwell in safety and in peace. Such is the way you bless your own! Thank you, Father. It is a wonderful thing to be able to say, "You are my Rock!"

Things To Ponder

It is little wonder that we read, "All in the temple cry "Glory!" We join our voices with theirs. We bow in worship with the angels above.

Psalm 30

"Putting Problems Into Perspective"

Psalm 30

A Psalm.
A Song for the dedication of the temple (house) of David.

1 I will exalt you, O Lord,
  for you lifted me out of the depths
  and did not let my enemies gloat over me.

2 O Lord my God, I called to you for help,
  and you healed me.
3 O Lord, you brought me up from the grave;
  you spared me from going down into the pit.

4 Sing to the Lord, you saints of his; praise his holy name.

5 For his anger lasts only a moment,
  but his favor lasts a lifetime;
weeping may remain for a night,
  but rejoicing comes in the morning.

6 When I felt secure, I said,
  I will never be shaken."
7 O Lord, when you favored me,
  you made my mountain stand firm;
  but when you hid your face, I was dismayed.

8 To you, O Lord, I called; to the Lord I cried for mercy:

9 "What gain is there in my destruction,
  in my going down into the pit?
  Will the dust praise you?
  Will it proclaim your faithfulness?

10 Hear, O Lord, and be merciful to me; O Lord, be my help.

11 You turned my wailing into dancing;
    you removed my sackcloth and clothed me with joy.
12 that my heart may sing to you and not be silent.

O Lord my God, I will give you thanks forever.

NIV

Psalm 30

Putting Problems Into Perspective
A Song At The Dedication of The House of David

I. The Dramatic Deliverance. "I Cried … He Answered!" *"I will exalt you, O Lord … O Lord my God, I called to you for help …" (v 1, 2).*

A. You lifted me up *"out of the depth"*
B. You delivered me *"and did not let my enemies gloat over me"*
C. You healed me *"when I called to you for help"*
D. You spared me *"you brought me up from the grave; you spared me from going down into the pit"*

II. The Lessons Learned. He Calls On The Saints (Faithful Ones) To Join Him in Praise. *"Sing to the Lord, you saints of his; praise His holy name" (v 4).*

A. It is important to put the problems of the moment into the perspective of a lifetime. *"For his anger lasts only a moment, but his favor lasts a lifetime" (v 5).*
B. We should keep in mind that trouble is usually short-lived. *"weeping may remain for a night, but rejoicing comes in the morning" (v 6).*\

III. The Predictable Pathway. Life is Filled With Ups and Downs.

A. We often lose sight of God when times are prosperous, and everything seems to go well. *"When I felt secure, I said, "I will never be shaken." O Lord, when you favored me, you made my mountain stand firm" (v 6, 7).*
B. Suddenly things go wrong, and it seems like God turns away. We feel alone and alienated. *"… but when you hid your face, I was dismayed." (v 7).*
C. Then we cry out for help to God. *"To you, O Lord, I called; to the Lord I cried for mercy" (v 8).*
D. We reason with the Lord. If I'm dead, how can I praise you? *"What gain is there in my destruction, in my going down into the pit? Will the dust praise you? Will it proclaim your faithfulness?" (v 9).*
E. We continue our desperate cry for help. *"Hear, O Lord, and be merciful to me: O Lord be my help" (v 10).*
F. The answer comes! Lord, you have made all the difference!

1. You changed my sadness into gladness. *"You turned my wailing into dancing;"*
2. You turned my; mourning into merriment. *"you removed my sackcloth and clothed me with joy" (v 11).*

IV. The Joyful Celebration."... *that my heart may sing to you and not be silent. O Lord my God, I will give you thanks forever" (v 12).*

Psalm 30

Putting Problems Into Perspective

The title of this psalm suggests that it was written for the dedication of the house of David. The truth is, we are really not sure what "house" is in view, and all we need to know is that David on this occasion was remembering a time when God rescued him from a near death experience. He reflects on what the experience taught him about putting problems that we face into perspective, and how our extremity can be God's opportunity to work in our behalf. It also could be an Old Testament commentary on the second beatitude, *"Blessed are those who mourn, for they shall be comforted" (Matthew 5:4)* Mourning signals need. We mourn the way things are in order to experience what they were meant to be. When we come to the end of ourselves, then we find ourselves, and our true comfort in God.

First, David shares a time when the Lord wrought a remarkable deliverance, bringing help and healing to him in his desperate condition.

The Dramatic Deliverance. "I Cried … He Answered!" *"I will exalt you, O Lord … O Lord my God, I called to you for help" (v 1, 2)*

That his plight was desperate is seen by the phrases he uses to describe it, "the depths," "the grave," and "into the pit." He was about as low as one could get, and still be alive. He declares the Lord …

+ lifted me up (like a bucket from a well)
+ delivered me
+ healed me
+ spared me

The Lord lifted him up and out of his woeful condition. He calls on "the saints" (the faithful ones), perhaps the Levites, to join him in praise to the Lord, and he reflects on the lessons he learned from the experience.

The Lessons Learned.

He wished to share with his worshipping friends a couple of valuable lessons learned from his experience.

The first thing he learned was that **the problems of the moment need to be put into the perspective of a lifetime.** *"For his anger lasts only a moment, but his favor lasts a lifetime" (v 5).* We are prone to say, "Time heals all wounds." Or again, "This too will pass!" These can be trite, but true. I am reminded that the apostle Paul tells us to take even a longer view, placing the sufferings of this present time in the continuum of eternity. *"I consider that our present sufferings are not worth comparing with the glory that will be revealed in us" (Rom. 8:18).* Or yet again, *"For our light and momentary troubles are achieving for us an eternal glory that far outweighs them all" (2 Corinthians. 4:17).*

The second insight is related to the first. We should keep in mind **that trouble is usually short-lived.** *"… weeping may remain for a night, but rejoicing comes in the morning" (v 6).* Sometimes a good night's sleep yields a better perspective. The "dark soul of the night" gives way to the dawning of new day. Even the act of weeping can be therapeutic. The Preacher reminds us, *"Sorrow is better than laughter: for by the sadness of the countenance the heart is made better."* Robert Browning Hamilton's poem, *Along the Road* expresses this thought:

> I walked a mile with pleasure,
> She chattered all the way,
> But left me none the wiser
> For all she had to say.
>
> I walked a mile with sorrow
> And ne'er a word said she;
> But oh, the things I learned from her
> When sorrow walked with me.

The Predictable Pathway.

Next, David traces a predictable pathway that most traverse sometime in their lifetime. Life, he suggests, has its ups and downs. He reminds us that **we tend to lose sight of God when times are prosperous,** and everything seems to be going well. *"When I felt secure, I said, 'I will never be shaken.' O Lord, when you favored me, you made my mountain stand firm" (v 6,7).* There seems to be a touch of pride and self-sufficiency here. When things are going great, we often lose our sense of trustful dependence on God.

Then suddenly and unexpectedly things go wrong, and it seems like God has turned away from us. *"… but when you hid your face, I was dismayed." (v 7).* We feel very much alone and alienated.

Then, when we don't know what to do, and we come to the end of our own resources, we cry out for help to God. *"To you, O Lord, I called; to the Lord I cried for mercy" (v 8).* As the old song put it, "Where could I go but to the Lord!" When King Jehoshaphat and his people were up against it, a great army advancing on them. He went before the Lord, and cried, "Lord, neither know we what to do, but our eyes are upon you."

David even offers reasons to the Lord why he should come to his rescue. If I'm dead, he argues, how can I praise you? *"What gain is there in my destruction, in my going down into the pit? Will the dust praise you? Will it proclaim your faithfulness?" (v 9).* So he continues his desperate cry for help. And the answer comes, and everything changes!

+ You changed my sadness into gladness! *"You turned my wailing into dancing."*

+ You turned my mourning into merriment! *"You removed my sackcloth and clothed me with joy!" (v 11).*

For Jeremiah, the Weeping Prophet, it was the direct opposite, because of the disobedience of the people and impending captivity, *"The joy of our heart is ceased; our dance is turned into mourning" (Lam. 5:15).* Praise God that our Lord Jesus did not come to condemn us for our sin, but to bear it on himself in his own body on the accursed tree. His stated mission in Isaiah's words was *"to proclaim the acceptable year of the Lord"* and *"to comfort all that mourn; To appoint unto them that mourn in Zion, to give unto them beauty for ashes, the oil of joy for mourning, the garment of praise for the spirit of heaviness" (Is. 61:2, 3).*

The Joyful Celebration.

The psalmist cannot keep silent. His heart is filled with thanksgiving and praise. *"… that my heart may sing to you and not be silent. O Lord my God, I will give you thanks forever" (v 12).*

Father, please teach me to put the problems of the moment into the perspective of a lifetime, and to realize that trouble is usually short lived. I have traveled the predictable pathway, and you have shown me the way out of difficulty into delight. My heart must "sing to you and not be silent." I will give you thanks forever.

978-0-595-47171-3
0-595-47171-4